How to Care for Pet Rabbits and Guinea Pigs

The Essential Guide to Ownership, Care, and Training for Beginners - 2 **Books in 1**

Dave Josephson

ISBN: 9798539151904

Table of Contents

Book 1; How to Care for Pet Rabbits

The beginners Guide to House Rabbit Ownership

About this Book

How to Care for Pet Rabbit is divided into three parts made up of several chapters relating to the specific topic covered in each part.

Part One. About the World of Rabbits

This part helps you to discover whether a rabbit is right for your lifestyle. You will learn important facts about rabbit personality and why living with them can be so much exciting.

Part Two. Pet Rabbit Care and Behavior

In this part, you will get information about different breeds and how to choose the right one. You will also discover how to care for them in terms of proper housing and feeding for a long healthy life. Rabbits obviously don't speak human language, but like all animals, they have their own unique language. This section helps you to know more about this important phenomenon that promotes robust relationship with your affectionate pet.

Part Three: Common Rabbit Diseases.

Because your pet rabbits are susceptible to illness, their healthcare is an important issue. This section contains rabbit general health information and overviews of their most common health problems. In this part, you can find out how to identify common rabbit health issues, how to prevent them, and when to take a trip to the vet.

Part One. About the World of Rabbits

This part helps you to discover whether a rabbit is right for your lifestyle. You will learn important facts about rabbit personality and why living with them can be so much exciting.

1 The Benefits of Owning a Pet Rabbit

Rabbits are adorable little creatures with distinctive personalities. They are a great first pet to own. Not only are they easy to care for, they are extremely affectionate and charming. You can't get bored when together with a rabbit; their charming and warm temperament brings a lot of joy and entertainment to any home. They are interactive and provide real sense of purpose and companionship for families. They offer your home many of the same benefits any pet dog or cat would. If you desire a low maintenance, warm and fascinating pet for your home, try a rabbit. They are the perfect companion for families for a variety of reasons.

Here are some great benefits of owning a pet rabbit.

Rabbits Are Quiet Pets- Rabbits are generally very quiet pets; they don't bark or make loud noises like dogs do. If you are in an apartment building with sensible neighbors you won't get complaints about noise or disturbance in any form. Also, if you are a light sleeper and want peace and quietness then a bunny is an ideal pet choice for you. They won't disturb nor bother you unnecessarily. The only time rabbits will make noise is when they are hurt or terrified by something, and they will only squeal to alert you. They provide a lot of comforts and are established forms of positivity during times of stress for anyone.

Rabbits are Clean- Rabbits are relatively clean animals and can be toilet trained. They aren't as messy as many small pets. You can train them to go to the toilet in a litter tray for easy cleaning of their living area. Also, they naturally would groom themselves to keep clean. Although, some do need regular grooming, generally, they appear neat and cute naturally.

Amazing Personality- Rabbits have distinct personalities. Their charisma comes out as you get to know them. They can be charming, affectionate and entertaining. But just like other pets, some rabbits may be playful while others may be shy and reserved, they have different personalities. Sometimes they may want to be alone and other times they want to socialize with people and want interaction. Just make sure you select the one that meets your expectations and lifestyle while adopting them as pets. The good thing is that there are so many different types of rabbits to choose from. While each rabbit is a unique individual, many of these breeds share certain qualities and characteristics in terms of appearance and temperament.

Rabbits Produce Great Compost- Rabbits are excellent compost producers. They will give you fertilizers that you can use in your organic garden. You can use their waste directly as fertilizer, or you can put them into great compost and use. Also, their poop is easy to clean up, unlike other pet animals. Their poops are tiny solid balls that don't have any serious odor and can be easily swept up with a broom or vacuumed. Once they are toilet trained you don't have to clean their poop as much.

Rabbit can Get Bond closely- Rabbits can get closely bond like cats and dogs with their owners. When you interact regularly with them they can get to know you well. They can recognize you by your voice and sight and even respond appropriately to your command and gestures. They are a wonderful companion that is fairly easy to train.

Rabbits need Less Space than other House Pets- If you live in an apartment with lesser space and you desire a cuddly pet, a rabbit might just be ideal for you. They don't require large space like other pets such as cats and dogs. They are low maintenance animals. A space that is large enough for them to stretch out, accommodate a little pan in one corner and a feeding corner can serve them well. Also, they don't need to be walked; however, they do need a couple of hours exercise a day to keep happy and healthy.

Sense of Responsibility- Owning a pet rabbit gives you a sense of responsibility. It's a good way to keep you busy and focus on something which is very beneficial to your health. For kids, a pet rabbit is a great way to teach responsibility. When children are attached to care for your rabbit you are developing their sense of responsibility. Also, you are helping them to develop important social skills. You are teaching them to look outside of themselves and to show empathy for others. Children who grow up in a home with pets benefit greatly in the area of their emotional development.

Their Fur can be turned into Fiber- There are several breeds of rabbits that produce enough wool that can be harvested and turned into fiber just like sheep's wool. The angora rabbit is a good example.

Health Benefits- Owning a pet comes with a lot of health benefits. It helps both mental and emotional health. It can decrease stress and anxiety. You can get a lot of benefits from stroking and playing with your rabbits like many other pets. Rabbits are wonderful creature who can make you forget about bad moments or the usual worries. No matter the situation, rabbit will brighten it up with their hoping and running around your home.

2 Things to Know Before Getting a Pet Rabbit

Rabbits are affectionate animals and can make great additions to any household. They really do make wonderful pets, but it's imperative to recognize that like any other pet such as cats and dogs, they also require a lot of care. Keeping them comes with a lot of responsibilities. They need a lot of time, effort and money to ensure they are kept healthy and lively. Here are some essential things you need to know if you're considering owning a pet rabbit.

They're not good pets for young children

Children love playing with rabbits. Some people even see them as children's pets, but rabbits may be less excited with a small kid as their primary caretaker. They are often frightened by the excited shouting and sudden movements of young children. Every child would love a hoppy little bunny to call their own but sometimes they may not respond well to lots of cuddles. Most rabbits do not like to be picked up and held. Improper handling can cause serious or fatal injuries. They can be easily hurt or traumatized due to their fragile nature. Therefore, their interaction with children should be supervised when being handled by them, most especially children under 8 years old. The good thing is that rabbits can be faithful and affectionate companions with proper care and understanding. They can develop a strong emotional bond with their caregiver, even children.

Rabbits can live for 10 to 12 years

House rabbits are not short-term pets. Rabbits can live up to 8 to12 or more years old. This may be the most vital thing to know when it comes to pet rabbits because they are delicate prey pets that require time, attention, special diet, and expensive vet care. Although, they are pretty much the cutest thing that can grace your household with love and amusing relief; they require a sizable degree of daily and weekly care over their life span. You should get prepared for a long companionship. The latter part of this book shows you how to care for these wonderful creatures.

Rabbits require unique medical care

Rabbits are not like cats and dogs; they have their own needs and require special knowledge and care. They have their own specialized vets. In the veterinary term, they are considered exotic animals. Their care, medication, and surgery are delicate; they are precise matters that should not be handled by just anybody. They need specialists who know about rabbits very well. Also, it is essential you take your rabbit for regular vet checkups. It is important to check their teeth, ears, eyes, and gut to make sure they are in good health.

Socialization

Rabbits are naturally social and inquisitive animals; they enjoy regular interaction and enrichment. They can equally get bored like humans, so they need play, exercise, and mental stimulation.

You will need to provide them space to exercise and plenty of toys to keep them entertained. They need social interaction with humans and enjoy the company of one another. They love the company and become lonely and depressed when they don't have companions of their own kind.

Having a pair can help ensure they don't become lonely. However, care must be taken when putting them together. Rabbits can start to become sexually active from three months of age. You have to consider spaying/neutering them to prevent *accidental pregnancies* and breeding against your wish.

Self-Grooming

Rabbits are relatively clean animals. They will naturally self-groom to keep themselves clean. If they are in the company of other rabbits they will groom each other. You may not need to bath your rabbit as it can lead to shock which can create other health-related issues. Rabbits benefit from regular brushing, mainly when they are shedding their fur. They go through shedding cycles a couple of times a year. In this case, you have to brush your rabbit to remove all the excess fur. However, some breeds of rabbit with a heavy wool cover, such as Angoras, will require regular shearing which should be performed by a professional groomer.

Rabbits are crepuscular

Rabbits keep their own time; they are most active at dusk and dawn. People often wonder whether rabbits sleep during the day or at night. And the answer is neither. But they normally rest during midday. Once they are weaned it's hard to see them falling into an extended sleeping hour. They are adaptable and will adjust to whatever schedule you keep.

Their nails and teeth never stop growing

The teeth on a rabbit grow constantly hence they need something to chew on. If their teeth stop grinding normally, they may find eating painful and starve. Like humans, their nails grow continually and need a trim about every six weeks. Long and unkempt nails can get snagged on things causing accidents.

Other Facts

The only place bunnies actually sweat is on the pads of their feet. They actually have five toenails in their front paws and four toe nails in their back paws. They are born furless with their eyes closed.

Rabbits can be litter trained

Rabbits can be litter trained. They are creatures of habitat who can get used to a routine and stick to it rigidly. Rabbits usually choose to toilet in corners where they have gone before. You can take advantage of this natural inclination by setting up a litter box in that spot. Or set up the liter pan near their food bowls and hay feeder and put a thin layer of rabbit-safe, recycled newspaper pellet litter at the bottom of the litter pan. To pin them to that spot and encourage good litter box habit, put hay on top of the litter. Bunnies like to eat hay and poop at the same time.

You have to consider the type of your rabbit to adopt the style and size of the litter pan that is most suitable. The larger your rabbit, the larger the litter pan you'll use. Healthy younger rabbits do well with high-back litter pans, but senior rabbits or those that are deformed might need a lower litter pan

You need to Rabbit-proof the rabbit's access area in your house

This is the most crucial part of preparing for your new pet. Naturally, Rabbits love to chew and dig, they will try to chew everything in reach. You'll need to rabbit-proof their access area in your home to protect your belongings. You have to prepare adequately for this as you are getting ready to welcome your new guest to minimize the damage to both your rabbit and your property.

Don't allow them access to the plants in your house, if you don't want your plants eaten. Besides, some plants could be toxic to your rabbit.

Furthermore, block their access to exposed cables, door frames, loose bits of carpeting, anything made out of wood or just keep them out of their reach at all times.

Spaying and Neutering

If you plan to keep a mixed-sex pair of pet rabbits, they both need to be spayed or neutered so that they can live together happily. Spayed and neutered buns are less prone to a variety of diseases and tend to live reasonably longer than rabbits who haven't been spayed or neutered. It makes them better companions and develops a loving and sustainable bond.

Your male pet rabbits can be castrated at any age. But it's best to have them castrated as soon as their testicles begin to form when they are between 2-3 months old. Spaying can be performed at a similar age, but the uterus is very small at this point, and the age of 4-5 months is usually preferred. Whatever be the case, it should be done before the rabbit is 2 years old to get the advantage of the prevention of disease. Neutering operation seems straightforward and recovery time is quite quick, provided there are no complications. But it's important you consult a rabbit savvy vet.

Rabbits produce two types of *poops*

Rabbits produce two types of poops —one is soft, dark, undigested food material. The other is a hard, light-colored pellet made of feces. To gain nutrients from undigested food, rabbits will re-ingest these poops to further digest the material.

Rabbits are Prey Animals

Rabbits are prey animals. They are low on the food chain in the wild. Pet rabbits face many dangers from predators if kept outdoors. They could be opened to attacks from dogs, raccoons, cats (both domestic and wild), snakes, wolves, and birds of prey such as hawks, owls, falcons, and eagles. They are sensitive to the predator's attack. They can die or fall into shock mode simply from the stress of smelling or hearing a predator nearby. This means they have different requirements and behaviors from your pet cat or dog. You will learn more about how to protect your rabbits from predators in the later part of this book.

Confinement is not a punishment for rabbits

Rabbits enjoy confinement. They are quite comfortable in their living area which could be a cage or a corner of your house or room. The only thing is that make sure they are actively engaged. Give them something to toss and chew when in their living area so they can exercise their teeth and satisfy their curiosity. It is equally important to let them have time to exercise & stretch occasionally.

Rabbits don't tolerate Frequent Changes in their diet

Rabbits' don't want nor require frequent changes in their diet. They have a delicate and unique digestive system that can be easily upset. If you need to change their feed, gradually increase the percentage of the new item to see if it agrees with your rabbit. You will learn more about feeding your rabbit for better health in part two.

3 Common Terminology for Rabbit

Rabbit care has a unique language and terms. Here is a quick list of the terminology you should know as a new house rabbit owner.

Agouti: A fur color pattern where each individual hair alternates different color

Albino: A term used for a white rabbit with pink eyes.

ARBA: The American Rabbit Breeders Association =umbrella national rabbit leading organization.

Binkies: A term used when a bunny is running and jumping around in a very happy fashion.

Breed: A breed is a type of rabbit

Breeder: A person who owns and mates rabbits to produce baby rabbits.

Breeding: The process of doe and buck

Buck: A male rabbit

Cecotropes: Rabbit poo which looks more like a little bunch of shiny dark brown which they eat directly from their anus as it comes out to get additional nutrition and beneficial bacteria.

Commercial breed: A term used to describe the breed of rabbit that was developed for meat production.

Crown: The part of a rabbits head between the ears and behind the brow

Dam: A term used for the mother of a particular rabbit.

Doe: A female rabbit

Fryer: This is a term used for when a rabbit reaches butchering age or size.

Gestation: The time it takes from when the doe is impregnated to when she gives birth. It is usually 28-31 days

Herd: The name used to describe a group of rabbits.

Hole: The rabbit's home or cage

Hutch or cage: A special type of outdoor rabbit housing

Intermediate: A rabbit that more than 6 months but less than 8 months old.

Junior: A Rabbit under 6 months of age.

Kindling: Term used to mean giving birth to baby rabbits.

Kit: A baby rabbit

Litter: A term used for a group of rabbit kits from the same mother born at the same time (one birth)

Molt: A coat that is shedding and out of condition.

Nest Box or kindling box: A box provided for does to make a nest and have babies. The box will hold the kits and keep them warm and protected.

Palpation: A term used to describe feeling for the developing embryos within the abdominal cavity of the pregnant rabbit.

Rabbitry: Generally called such for people with any amount of rabbits who are raising them for exhibition, breeding, pets, meat, etc.

Roaster: A term used to describe a rabbit older and larger than a fryer.

Senior: A rabbit over 6 months of age

Sewer: A term used for an old and large rabbit with tough meat.

Sexing: A term used for the technique of checking the bunnies' genitals to determine if it is male or female.

Solid: A color of a rabbit that is covering the entire body

Variety: Term used to describe the color of a rabbit

Weaned: Refers to a baby rabbit that is no longer with the mother - it is on its own eating and drinking.

Weaning: A term used to describe the separation of baby rabbits from their nursing mother. This is usually done when the baby is around the age of 6-8 weeks.

The class age group of the rabbit is Junior, Intermediate or Senior.

4 Rabbit Housing

Owning a pet is a great decision and part of having a pet rabbit is making sure they have a great home to live in. It is crucial for you to get the environment right for your pet and also providing them with a safe and secure home. A rabbit's home base should be a special place where she can feel safe and secure. The good thing is that your rabbit can be raised outdoors or indoors. They can live in cages place indoors or outdoors. They can as well live freely with you inside the house. Whatever your choice, all should have enough space to exercise and provide shelter from severe weather conditions and predators. While different rabbit breeds differ in size and weight, they all require similar features in their housing. Here are some basic guidelines for consideration while choosing or designing a house for your rabbits.

Ventilation

The housing should be an enclosed space that has proper ventilation, lighting, cooling systems, and heating. Heating and ventilation are critical because rabbits do not tolerate extreme weather conditions very well. They are prone to heatstroke and other environmental induced dangers.

Easy To Clean

You need to keep their cages clean regularly or else they will end up getting sick. Therefore, you should consider getting a cage that is easy to clean and maintain. Make sure it has easy access to bedding, food, and litter. Flooring should be built and kept to minimize injury or distress to your pet rabbits. They should not be placed in cages with complete wire floors. This may be too hard on their feet. However, if the bottom is made from a wire, you need to protect their feet by placing any solid flooring item on part of the floor area. Alternatively, you can use cages with slatted plastic floors, which seems more comfortable.

Portability

If you plan to purchase premade cages, another thing to consider is the portability of the cage in case you need to move around with your pet rabbit. Cages with caster wheels can be easily moved about. Lightweight folding designs cages are equally good; it allows you to easily dismantle and carry along.

An access door

Access door should be located such that you can reach into different areas of the cage. In addition, it should be large enough for the rabbit to be taken in and out from the cage without banging the rabbit against the sides of the opening. And also it should be big enough to move the litter box in and out. It should also contain a latch that the rabbit cannot accidentally open or forced open by some determined predators.

A Nest Box

If you plan to breed your rabbits, a nest box is necessary. It provides seclusion for the doe and protection for the litter. It should be placed in the cage prior to kindling (birth). The nest box should be closed with a small opening on top for the doe to enter. Also, it should be able to accommodate the doe and her litter but small enough to keep the litter close together. If you don't intend breeding your rabbit, you don't need to worry about this requirement.

Size

The size of the cage will depend on the number of pets that you have as well as the space available in your house. As we know larger rabbits will require more space than smaller rabbits. Therefore, space allowances should be adjusted relative to the size of your rabbit. But in general, the length of the cage should be at least 4-6 times the length of the rabbit when stretched out and twice as wide as the rabbit. Anything smaller can make your rabbit struggle to survive in the pen.

Also, the pen should contain enough space for a litter box, food bowl, water source, and toys. There should be a minimum amount of space for the rabbit to lie down for a nap, sit upright without crouching, stand to see outside the cage or pen and move around comfortably.

Other Important Considerations

A cage with a side/front opening door will help the bunny to hop in and out at playtime. You should also consider the top opening panel for easy cleaning.

If you desire to provide your rabbit with a larger space than its hutch/cage when you deem it necessary, consider a pet pen or a children's playpen. This will make them confined to an enclosed area and secure them from predators. You could attach it to the hutch/cage to give them a larger free area to exercise and play.

Location

Once you've selected the right housing for your pet rabbits, you'll need to determine the specific place in your home they will live. The location of the cage in your home is crucial to the wellbeing of your rabbit. Here are some factors to consider:

Temperature: The ideal temperature range for rabbits is approximately 65-75 degrees Fahrenheit. Therefore, the cage should be located away from strong heat sources such as direct sun, radiator, wood stoves, fireplaces and heating vents. Remember, they are particularly susceptible to heat stroke.

Also, place the cages in a draft-free area on an elevated surface. Rabbits don't do well under humid conditions. Dampness promotes the growth of mold in their hay and bedding and can make them more predisposed to various diseases.

Activity level: Rabbits enjoy being near family activity and benefit immensely from more attention and regular interaction with their owner. A family room or living room works well, but make sure they have a hidden place to retreat if they need some quiet time.

Noise: Rabbits have very strong and sensitive hearing system. Their cages should not be placed near loud noise or a high traffic area in the home.

Cage Construction Material

Rabbit hutches can be made using a wide range of materials. The most important thing is that any materials must be durable and easily cleaned. A plastic designed cage provides enough air and light into the cage and makes it easier for you to clean and keep an eye on your pet. Wooden rabbit cages are equally good but may be difficult to clean. Also, if the wood is not treated, fungus and moss will be an issue, most especially if your rabbit is not litter box trained.

As earlier stated, rabbits are prone to heat stress, therefore, a metal cage/hutch or shed is not recommended as it can cause overheating.

Part Two. Pet Rabbit Care and Behavior

In this part, you will get information about different breeds and how to choose the right one. You will also discover how to care for them in terms of proper housing and feeding for a long healthy life. Rabbits obviously don't speak human language, but like all animals, they have their own unique language. This section helps you to know more about this important phenomenon that promotes robust relationship with your affectionate pet.

5 Guide to the Best Rabbit Breeds

Choosing a rabbit breed that is ideal for your specific need could be one of the most critical yet exciting parts of your pet rabbit adventure. Rabbits are intelligent creatures like most other animals; they tend to have their own unique characters and personalities. There are many different breeds that you can potentially choose from. Presently American Rabbit Breeders Association (ARBA) recognizes about 50 breeds.

Each breed has its own unique lifestyle requirements. Only make sure you choose the correct breeds that suit your lifestyle. Some are fluffy with thick, soft coats while some are slim and sleek. Any of them can make a good pet, but in making your choice you need to consider the size of the rabbit and the amount of care it requires.

We have listed some of the best rabbit's breeds and provide some important information about each to help you make a good choice and find a perfect companion.

Gender

Another important thing that usually bothers the mind of a new pet owner is the sex of the rabbit to be adopted. Either sex can make a good pet. They will only need to be altered to get the best out of them. Unaltered rabbit is likely to spray urine upon reaching sexual maturity. Also, they are prone to some diseases and can be more aggressive.

Small Rabbit Breeds (*mature weight usually less than six pounds*).

American Fuzzy Lop Rabbit

The American fuzzy lop is believed to have originated from the United States of America. They come in a variety of fur colors which always appear unkempt due to its texture. They do require an owner who is committed to grooming their coats regularly to keep them in good shape than what non-wool breeds need. Because of this special requirement, they may not be a good pet for people who don't have time for grooming.

The American Fuzzy Lop has a short, broad, compact, well-balanced and well-rounded body that appears muscular which weighs 3-4 ponds as an adult. They have a short and flat muzzle similar to that of a cat; their ears do not stand erect, but rather lop along the side of their face.

Britannia Petite Rabbit

The Britannia petite rabbit as the name suggests was developed in the United Kingdom in the 19th century. They are small rabbit breeds weighing about 2.5 pounds when fully grown. They are energetic and live between 5 to 8 years and in some cases 10 years. They are slender and come in a variety of colors. While they are inquisitive and friendly, they can be anxious and excitable and may need considerably more exercise than some other breeds. They are best suitable for gentle and calm families that have enough space for them to have a nice run and play session. They do not require any special grooming.

Dutch Rabbit

The Dutch rabbit which is also known as **_Brabander_** or **_Hollander_** **_was_** developed in England in the 1830s. This pretty little Dutch rabbit is one of the oldest domesticated rabbit breeds in the world. They are popular because of their wonderful calm friendly disposition and manageable size with fur that does not require any special grooming. The Dutch rabbit is a very popular breed for show and also raised as pets. The breed is recognized by both the British Rabbit Council and American Rabbit Breeders Association. It's characteristic color pattern make it easily identifiable. It is smaller in size, but not a dwarf breed. They have compact and well-rounded head and body. Their back legs seem longer than the front legs like other rabbit breeds. They are adaptable and versatile, and easy to train. Their striking colors are a delight to watch, and the coat is easy to maintain. The Dutch rabbits can become depressed if it spends too much time in its cage therefore socializing is important to make them lively.

Dwarf Hotot rabbit:

Dwarf Hotot rabbit originated in Germany. They are a small rabbit breed that weighs between 2.5 to 3.5 pounds once fully grown. They are quiet, affectionate, social, and delightful and make good indoor pet companions and exhibition rabbits. Their coats are white with a contrast black eye marking. They have a compact body, with a round, well-filled head and short neck. Their ears are short and thick. In addition to their delightful appearance, they also have a friendly personality that makes them a great pet for families and any first-time pet owners. They can live for between 7 and 10 years and does very well in any enclosure indoors and outdoors.

Havana Rabbit:

The Havana rabbit breed originated in Holland. It is a lovely rabbit breed that is recognized by the American Rabbit Breeders Association in five different color types. They have a calm and affectionate temperament which makes them a great pet for first-time owners. Also, they are a lovely show rabbit with a great shiny coat and good body conformation. They weigh in at about 5 pounds and have an average lifespan of 5 to 8 years.

Himalayan Rabbit

The Himalayan rabbit is both one of the oldest, and also one of the calmest breeds in personality. Its origins are still primarily unknown. The breed is a good choice for families with children to have as pets. They are quite easy to maintain either indoors or outdoors which makes them a good choice for a novice rabbit owner. The Himalayan rabbit's fur is short and soft, making it remarkably easy to care for. They typically weigh between 2 to 4 pounds as adults and have an average lifespan of 7 to 10 years.

Jersey Wooly Rabbit

The Jersey Wooly rabbit originated from New Jersey in the 1980s. They are tiny rabbit breeds that have long fluffy wool. On average, they generally weigh up to 3 pounds once full grown but can weigh as little as 1 pound.

They have very long lifespans, they can live up to 10 years or more if they are neutered or spayed.

They are docile and do well with children which make them a great pet choice for first-time owners.

Lion head rabbit

The little Lion head rabbit breed originated from Belgium but was introduced in the U.S. in the '90s. It has wool mane encircling its head, reminiscent of a male lion as its name implies. They are small rabbits breed with compact rounded bodies and are considered to be an elegant breed. They are actually great little pets showing a lot of intelligence. They are calm, well-mannered and tolerant of children which make them a great choice for first-time pet owners, kids, and adults alike. This small bunny weighs about three pounds at maturity and can live up to 8 to 10 years.

Mini Lop Rabbit

The mini lop are known for their distinctive downward ears. They are very smart with friendly and playful personalities. They weigh up to 6 pounds and can live between 5 to 10 years. This friendly and playful personality makes them a good choice for families with kids. First-time rabbit owners may find this breed especially easy to care for. They don't require excessive grooming.

Netherland Dwarf Rabbit

This Netherlands dwarf rabbits are popular as both a pet and a show rabbit. They are one of the smallest breeds of rabbits that can adore your home. At an average weight of only 1.5 to 2.5 pounds, the Netherland dwarf can also live for about 9 to 12 years. They are not too difficult to maintain and make good house apartment pets, but may not be suitable for younger children due to their fragile nature. They come in a variety of fur colors and require little or no grooming.

The Angora rabbit

The **Angora rabbit** is one of the oldest types of domestic rabbits that are mainly bred for the long fibers of their coat, known as *Angora wool*. They are believed to have originated in Ankara, in present-day Turkey. It is well-known to have been brought to the south of **France** (Bordeaux) in 1723. They became a popular pet of the French royalty in the mid-18th century and later spread to other parts of Europe and the United States. Although they are usually bred for their fine long, soft wool which makes them so popular, they can also make great pets as well. The **American Rabbit Breeders Association** recognizes four different Angora rabbit breeds. These include the French angora, the English Angora, giant angora, and the satin angora. They are a high-maintenance breed that requires regular grooming to keep their fine wool in top shape. The wool of the Angora rabbit is used in making great sweaters. They are generally sweet-natured and curious and enjoy playtime with humans. They require love and attention, a clean habitat, plenty of food and water and some space to run around.

The Holland Lop

The Holland Lops are a low-maintenance, loving and adorable rabbit breed. Their lopped ears are one of their most unique features. They are one of the most popular rabbit breeds for city dwellers, both in the United States and around the world. The Holland lops are miniature rabbits that only weigh about 4 pounds once fully grown. They have a charming appearance with compact body shape and have a wide variety of coat colors.

Medium Rabbit Breeds *(mature weight usually between 6 and 9 pounds).*

Californian Rabbit

The Californian rabbit is a beautiful big white bunny developed by **George West** in Southern California in early 1920. They have a beautiful appearance. They are very active and playful. They enjoy playing and exploring and have a nice and easy-going temperament. Californian rabbit is widely raised as pets originally but can be raised for their fur value and meat production. It is a recognized breed by the American Rabbit Breeders Association. It is sweet, curious, gentle, and enjoys playtime with humans which makes it an ideal choice for any first-time rabbit owners. It has dense, shedding wool with a fluffy appearance and needs regular grooming, but not nearly as much as some other breeds. The

Californian rabbit can weigh up to 10 pounds when fully grown on average, and can live as long as 6 to 10 years.

Harlequin Rabbit

The Harlequin rabbit breeds originated from France. They are named after their unique-looking color combination and pattern. This feature makes them be referred to as the clown of the rabbit world. They are curious rabbits; they enjoy exploring their environment always. They can live for five to eight years and can weigh up to 10 pounds. Their active characters make them ideal playmates for children and first-time pet owners.

Satin Rabbit

The Satin Rabbit originated in the United States of America in the 1930s and is named for the unique bright and shiny texture of its wool. It is a medium to large breed with a unique look. It is quite a popular breed in the United States of America mainly adopted as a companion or pet rabbit breed as well as an exhibition rabbit breed. Satin rabbits can grow up to between 8 to 11 pounds on average. However, small Satins will only grow to about 6 pounds. They will need grooming about once a week or more with a soft brush. Kids will get along well with Satin rabbits, as they are considered to be mild and docile. Also, they are sociable and love to be around their caregivers.

Large Rabbit Breeds *(mature weight usually between 10 and 11 pounds).*
American Chinchilla Rabbit:

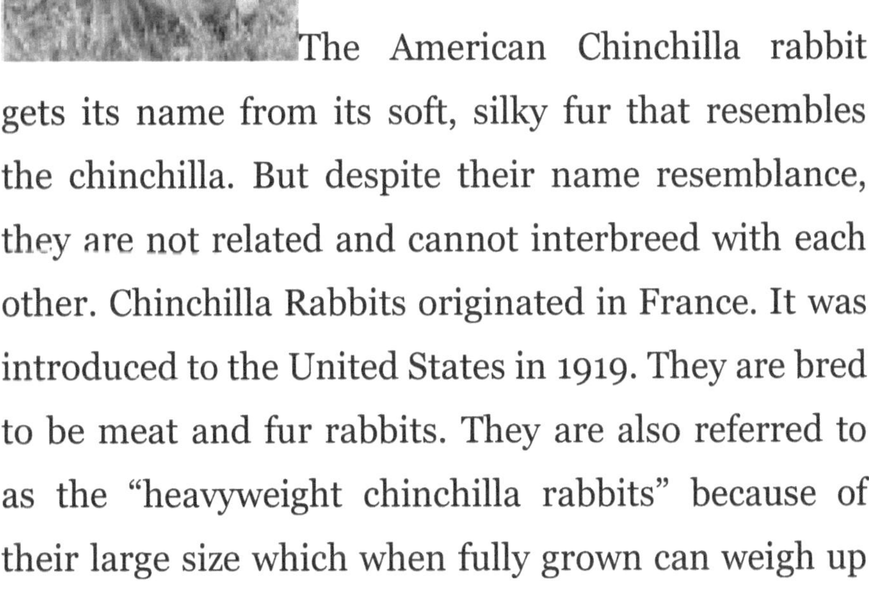The American Chinchilla rabbit gets its name from its soft, silky fur that resembles the chinchilla. But despite their name resemblance, they are not related and cannot interbreed with each other. Chinchilla Rabbits originated in France. It was introduced to the United States in 1919. They are bred to be meat and fur rabbits. They are also referred to as the "heavyweight chinchilla rabbits" because of their large size which when fully grown can weigh up

to 7 to 8 pounds. **They are naturally born** with a dark coat which changes with time as the animal grows older. They have a compact and stocky body, due to the fact that they were originally bred for both **meat and fur** purposes.

They are docile and sweet-natured breed demanding no strict requirements for care thereby making them a good choice for a novice rabbit owner. The American Chinchilla Rabbit does well in indoors or outdoors enclosures as long as the condition is favorable. They should not be exposed to extreme heat or cold. Cages should be large enough so the rabbit can easily stretch out. Outdoor cages should be raised a bit from the ground to protect them from predators.

English Lop Rabbit

The **English Lop** is a special breed of domestic rabbit that was developed in England in the 19th century through the process of selective breeding. It has distinctively long lop ears. The saggy ears are one of the characteristics of making it a very special breed. They are one of the oldest domestic rabbit breeds. They are very good pets for families and also for those who are interested in rearing them as show rabbit. They vary in color and they have high quality. Their lifespan is an average of five to six years. It is medium in size and may weigh up to 10.5 pounds. This type of breed of rabbit does not need consistent cleaning, as they are apt to prepare themselves well. In terms of taking care of them, you may occasionally make use of a slicker brush to remove vagrant hair and check their ears to prevent wax build-up. They can be kept either as an indoor or outdoor pet.

New Zealand Rabbit

The New Zealand rabbit comes from North America. They have cute chubby cheeks and are well known for their beautiful fur, which needs a modest amount of grooming occasionally. New Zealand rabbits make good pets if you are a first-time pet rabbit owner. They are affectionate, easy to handle and known for doing well with children. A full-grown adult will usually weigh up to 9 - 12 pounds. They are large and muscular can weigh up to 10 years if they are neutered.

Giant Breed (mature weight usually more than 12 pounds)

Continental giant rabbit

The continental giant rabbit also known as the German giant is a gentle giant breed of rabbit, a breed specifically for meat production. Continental rabbits can be traced back to the 16th century and originally came about as the offspring of Flemish giants. They are the biggest of the rabbit breeds. They are playful, docile, intelligent friendly, and easy to train. Normally they weigh between 16 to 25 pounds on average but can reach 40 pounds in some cases. The breed features a variety of colors which include light grey, steel grey, fawn, sandy, black and white. You will need to groom the coat regularly in order to keep them healthy. Also, large rabbit breeds may sometimes have trouble keeping themselves clean, particularly when they get older, so you will need to make efforts to ensure that your pet rabbit is kept clean.

Flemish Giant Rabbit

The Flemish Giant has many names. It is nicknamed the "Gentle Giant" for its uniquely docile personality and also the "universal rabbit" for its diverse purposes as a pet, meat, show, breeding, and fur domestic animal. It was bred in the 16th century near the city of Ghent, Belgium.

It is an impressively large giant breed that can weigh an astounding 14 pounds. It is a sturdy breed with docile personalities that is good for first-time owners, and in homes with indoor and outdoor enclosures. They have relatively low maintenance requirements but will need a little more space than smaller breeds because of their size. Occasional grooming will help eliminate shedding hair and keep their coat silky and soft.

Silver Fox Rabbit

The silver fox rabbit variety comes with a distinct, silver coat that resembles the pelt of the silver fox, hence the name. The breed was originally developed in Ohio, United States. The silver fox is a beautiful and rare breed of rabbits. They are easy to care for, calm and have a gentle personality which makes them a good pet for first-time rabbit owners. A silver fox rabbit has a lifespan of approximately 7 to 10 years and will weigh about 9 pounds on average.

The American checkered giant

The American checkered giant rabbit is a larger-sized rabbit breed that can weigh more than 11 pounds once fully grown. They are very active and energetic and are generally good-natured breed of rabbits with a relatively calm temperament. It's believed that the breed was developed in Europe either in France or Germany. The Checkered Giant has blue or black markings on either side of the body with a black or blue stripe running along from the base of their ears to their tail over the spine. Their fur is short, thick and tenderly soft with a semi-arched body. They have rings around the eyes, colored ears, cheek flashes and a butterfly-shaped marking on the nose with a wide head and broad ears that stand upright most of the time.

They do well either indoors or outdoors, but keeping them outdoor requires the provision of enclosures that are covered from the elements (sun and rain). These rabbits are typically used for show rather than for meat purposes, but they can also make brilliant pets for those looking for a sweet companion, as long as they are given warm affection and lots of outdoor playtimes.

6 Feeding Rabbits for a Long Healthy Life

Rabbits have an exclusive and delicate digestive system and you must take this into consideration when planning their feeding. Good nutrition reduces disease risk and boosts their immunity. Understanding your bunny dietary needs is crucial for long healthy life. A healthy diet should be high in fiber and fairly low in calories (especially fats and starches). A nice combination of hay, pellets, vegetables, as well as freshwater, will make your rabbit healthy and happy.

Hay

Hay is the most important factor in the diet of your rabbit. It should consist 75-80% of their diet. It provides the necessary fiber needed for good digestive health. It reduces the danger of hairballs and other blockages. It also helps in wearing their teeth for good dental health. Rabbit's teeth grow continually through their life, it is good they have something to chew to help keep them fill down.

Alfalfa hay with higher calories as well as calcium is good to feed young rabbits, but **should be avoided** for the average healthy, mature rabbit. Store hay in a cool, dry place to allow circulation and don't give damp hay.

Pellets

Pellets should mostly only contain a small portion of a house rabbit's diet. Make use of pellets that are high in fiber and low in protein (18% minimum fiber). And limit intake as your rabbit ages. Pellets with high protein content can lead to obesity and other health issues in rabbits. Give fresh pellets always and only buy enough for three months at a time. Store pellets in a closed container in a cool, dry place to avoid pellets becoming stale as your bunnies will reject stale pellets.

Vegetables and Fruits

Vegetables should be a good part of your rabbit's daily diet. *(5-15%).* Vegetables help balance out the nutritional needs in their diet. Make use of fresh dark green vegies and be sure it is free of pesticides before feeding them to your rabbits. Also, wash your vegetables thoroughly and feed them in small quantities and observe their reaction to know when to stop feeding them. Fruits can be given in small quantities because of the sugar content. Too much sugar consumption can make your rabbit fat.

Suggested vegetables

· Celery

· Basil

· Broccoli leaves (stems or tops)

· Lettuce – romaine or dark

· Cilantro

· Clover

· Collard greens

· Dandelion greens

· Collard greens

· Dill

· Mint

· Mustard greens

· Parsley

· Watercress

- Cabbage (red, green, Chinese)
- Carrot/beet tops
- Kale (sparingly)
- Green beans

Suggested fruits include:
- Strawberries
- Avocado
- Raspberries
- Cherries
- Cranberries
- Bananas
- Kiwi fruit
- Mango
- Pineapple
- Melons
- Apples (without seeds)
- Cactus fruit
- Strawberries (and leaves)

Nutrients Required by Rabbits

Rabbits require adequate amounts of **carbohydrates**, fiber, proteins, fats vitamins, minerals, and water to live and grow. They have the same basic nutritional **needs** as humans. However, too much or lack of any of the nutrients can cause problems for the rabbit.

Nutrients can be found in animal diet synthesized in the body, or taken in from the environment. Essential nutrients are nutrients that must be consumed in the diet because the animal cannot produce them in sufficient quantities while those they can synthesize to meet their needs or do not need from the diet are considered nonessential nutrients.

Water

Water is an essential ingredient in rabbit nutrition. It makes up more than half of the body mass of a rabbit. They can go many days without feed, but not so without water. The requirements vary depending on the prevailing environmental temperature, humidity, and activity level, among other factors. Give your rabbit **fresh water** every day. A typical rabbit may take about 10 milliliters of water per 100 grams of body weight. This means that an average-sized 5-pound rabbit takes at least 40 teaspoons of water a day. Nursing rabbits require an even higher water intake to meet the needs for milk production. Like any other animal, insufficient water intake can lead to dehydration in rabbits. It can also make rabbits developing urinary stones or crystals.

Ordinarily, rabbits get some water from the food they consume, especially in vegetables. If you suspect your rabbit does not seem to be getting enough, you can make the vegetables fairly wet when you give them.

Proteins

Proteins have an important structural role in the body of animals they are compounds comprised of amino acids. Rabbits require proteins in their diet for both essential and nonessential amino acids. Rabbits use lower quality proteins than most pets because they have a special means of meeting their needs. Their protein requirements increase during times of growth, pregnancy, or lactation (milk production).

Rabbit protein requirement varies with the growth stage. However, the minimum protein requirement for rabbit survival is about 8%. A non-producing adult requires 13 to 14 % protein and lactating does take 17 to 18% protein diet content.

Fiber

Fiber is crucially important for rabbit nutrition and health to prevent gastrointestinal disease and to provide a substrate for fermentation in the cecum. They need lots of fiber, both soluble and insoluble this is necessary for their guts to keep the contents moving along. Their diets should contain a minimum of 14 percent fiber. This may be higher in the diet of adult rabbits.

Carbohydrates

Carbohydrates diets are for energy and help boost the immune system. Carb overload can lead to an explosion of bacteria in the gut which can cause death to the rabbit quickly. A balance of carb and fiber will give a wonderful result.

Fats

Fats are an important part of cell membranes and serve several important functions in the body. Fats provide essential fatty acids and supply energy and also increase the energy content of the diet. The fat requirement of a pet rabbit is low, their diet should contain around 3 percent fat, but they can have slightly higher fat levels during lactation. Adding extra facts to a lactating doe diet will quickly boost her milk production. Too much fat can lead to obesity. Obesity can cause health problems and decrease the reproductive performance of your rabbits.

Minerals

Minerals have different functions in the body. Animals require about 22 different minerals in their diet. Calcium and phosphorus are vital minerals to consider in your rabbit's diet because of their role in the skeletal structure of the body.

The proportion of these minerals is determined by the life stage of your rabbit. Rabbits need higher levels of calcium and phosphorus during early growth to allow for bone development. Adult rabbits at maintenance need lower levels of calcium and phosphorus than at other life stages.

Calcium is provided from alfalfa which makes it more ideal for a rabbit diet. Phosphorus is generally provided by grain by-products such as wheat bran.

Vitamins

Rabbits require several different vitamins- which can be divided into fat-soluble and water-soluble vitamins. All these have their function in the body. Lack of it in the diet can cause illness, while excesses of some vitamins can also be toxic. Usually, a good quality diet will prevent vitamin imbalances and take care of all your rabbit's vitamin needs

7 Understanding of Rabbit's Body Language

Rabbits obviously don't speak human language, but like all animals, they have their own unique language. They communicate with each other and with their caregivers using a wide variety of body postures and a few vocalizations. As a pet owner, understanding, their body language, and common postures promote a good bond, which leads to security and enjoyment for both of you. Unlike cats and dogs, which make proper noises to get our attention, rabbits can't bark, meow, or purr. They have their own unique way of expressing different emotions such as anger, fear, happiness, or romance. You have to understand these signs to be able to effectively communicate with them. Rabbits can be restless when they want your attention. If it seems you don't understand one way they attempt to get your attention, they will try another way until you meet their request. The main thing is that your own rabbit's personality and body language can best be learned through careful observation of her behavior over time. Their behavior unfolds over time, and when you watch closely as you interact, you will learn the fascinating intricacies of their language. This will help you to work within their emotional limits and needs to become familiar with each other.

Communicating Through Body and Ears Positioning

Ears carriage and body posture is a tool rabbits use to communicate a lot. Research has shown that the position of their ears can be used to analyze their feelings.

Expectant position - Both ears up, they are attentive and expecting something to happen in a moment.

Spirited rabbit- If one ear is down while the other is up, it means the rabbit is aware of what is going on but feels the event may not warrant her full attention.

Pleasant rabbit- If both ears are in relaxing mode, it means pleasure- all is well at the moment.

Ear cleaning- If the rabbit is **shaking its ears followed by scratching inside them with a hind foot, it could be that the** rabbit has hair in its ears after a grooming session and trying to remove it. However, if she does this over and over, it could indicate ear mites' infection.

Excited rabbit- **If a little hop or jump follows ear shaking,** it means your rabbit is excited about something, and he is ready for play. This usually happens at the site of favorite feed.

Flattening- This is a situation where the rabbit makes itself as flat as possible, with the ears held tightly against the body. It is the rabbit's instinctive attempt to hide possibly against perceived danger. A pet rabbit in this posture mustn't be ignored. You should investigate what's causing this fearful behavior.

Angry rabbit— Rabbit stands on hind legs, and body visibly tensed, tail raised, and ears down and back. The head is forward with teeth sometimes visible. A rabbit in this position is angry and ready to fight. She may suddenly move forward and bite.

Relaxed or sleeping rabbit— Rabbit stretches out with hind feet and forefeet extended straight out from the body with eyes fully closed. Head may be raised or chin may rest between her forefeet.

Head shake— when a rabbit shakes her head while running and playing, it could mean that the rabbit is having a happy moment. **This can also occur when a rabbit** senses an unknown odor or has been disturbed or irritated.

Communication with Vocal Sounds And Touching

Lunging

This often occurs when you intrude on their living area or attempting to pick her up when she wants some privacy. It could also be that the rabbit is defending its territory because of unwanted threats.

Grunting

Grunts are rabbit's means of showing their anger or displeasure when they feel threatened. It is their usual response to unwanted behavior from humans or another rabbit. It may be followed by scratching or biting. Rabbits grunt when they want to be left alone or show their disapproval if they do not want to be touched or carried.

Tail wagging

Tail wagging in rabbits signifies disapproval or defiance. This usually happens when you are trying to enforce a rule she doesn't like.

Tooth-clicking

Tooth clicking indicates satisfaction and happiness. This occurs when a rabbit is in a relaxed mood moving her jaws back and forth, producing a soft grinding sound. A well-bonded rabbit will usually demonstrate this behavior when being petted/stroked and loved on. It can be compared to a purring cat.

Tooth-gnashing

This could signify intense pain, discomfort, or stress. It is often accompanied by a rabbit sitting hunched up in the corner of her living area, showing no interest in food or play, and passing few or no droppings. It merely means that all is not well with the rabbit, and you need to seek veterinary care immediately.

Yelling

Yelling can mean a rabbit is terrified, in great pain, or fearing for her life. Once you observe this, you should investigate the cause and take appropriate action immediately.

Honking

Soft, an almost inaudible sound usually in an unneutered male- it is a courting behavior. It is generally accompanied by circling.

Circling

This is a situation where rabbits lope slowly around the feet of the owner in circles to demand their attention. Circling is also perceived as a courting behavior.

Thumping

This is a loud tap of feet against the ground. Thumping is primarily an expression of fear and is equally used to communicate other things. They can thump to get attention, to express displeasure, or as a warning signal to others that they have seen or heard something.

Licking

This is a rabbit word for *liking. It is a rabbit* way of showing affection to their owner.

Spitting

This is another sound rabbits make when they are annoyed, angry, or frightened. It is sometimes called a hiss or a growl.

Squeak

Rabbits usually make this sound when they are afraid or hurt. It is a high-pitched sound that may occur singly or in succession.

Snort

Sometimes called a sniff. Rabbits make this sound to show annoyance or irritation. This sometimes occurs when you do something they dislike or present them with the food they don't want.

Other Communication Signals

Nose message

A rabbit's nose movement can be used to determine how interested they are in what's being observed and perceived. Rapid and faster wiggling indicate that the bunny is being attentive or agitated.

Rubbing noses with each other or on their caregiver is a sign of affection and trust.

Bunny enjoys sniffing to investigate. When they sniff you, it may be they are trying to find out something. Nose nudging can mean calling for attention.

Standing on hind legs

When rabbits stand on their hind feet, it may be that they are checking something out. They also used this posture for begging. Rabbits too do beg, they are worse than dogs when it comes to begging. They can stretch to any length to beg for sweets.

Flopping

Flopping is another way of expressing pleasure and happiness. A rabbit that exposes her belly suddenly is showing that you've earned her trust and approval. It indicates a relaxed and comfortable rabbit.

Laying head flat on the ground

Laying head flat on the ground is a way of s showing submission to the owner or another rabbit. It can also be that the rabbit is requesting petting or grooming from the owner.

Dancing

Rabbits are entertainers, they can dance. Dancing indicates happiness, contentment, and a high frame of mind.

Playing

Rabbits like playing a lot. They will explore, toss objects around, shred or chew toys and race wildly around the house. They can also jump on and off of the couch and act like a kid.

Territory Droppings

When a rabbit leaves droppings that are scattered and not in a pile, they are making a point. They are trying to mark their territory. Rabbits usually do this upon entering a new environment. If another rabbit lives around the same area, it may lead to serious consequences. She may want to defend her territory, which can lead to severe fighting.

Rattling cage bars

This usually occurs with rabbits that are not comfortable with their cage. It may be that the cage is strange to them and they are trying to escape. They may also do this to get your attention to rescue them.

8 Bonding With Your Rabbit

After getting ready the housing and all the accessories to welcome your bunny friend, there are some things you need to do to make the transition to living in your home easier. Don't expect your new pet to be instantly affectionate and playful right away. It will take her time to adjust to you and her new environment and feel safe. New environments make rabbits uneasy.

As your rabbit becomes accustomed to you and your home and loses her fear, her true personality will begin to unfold. You will begin to see behaviors that will delight and amuse you and a few that will surprise you. This depends partly on the age of your rabbit and the individual personality of your rabbit. Younger rabbits tend to be active and destructive than older ones.

Rabbits need good relationships to thrive in our homes. Bonding with them will help you learn about them and appreciate their unique personalities. One of the vital relationships a rabbit will ever cherish is with her immediate owner or caregiver. A good relationship is mutually satisfying and rewarding for both of you. It will help in so many ways to enhance her quality of life. But sound relationship won't just happen like the case of cats and dogs; it will take a more deliberate effort on your part as a pet owner. Rabbits are a prey animal that is timid and can be easily intimated. They are naturally **shy and distrustful** particularly in a new environment with unfamiliar faces. They are also easily scared by strange sounds, sudden movement or being held or picked up off the ground against their wish. This makes bonding with your rabbit a little more difficult than with a cat or dog but it could be easier if you start on the right foot.

As soon as you welcome your rabbit, first ensure that she is not afraid of you. Be patient, take things slowly and don't rush. Don't do anything to intimidate or scare her while you are providing for her initial essential needs. It may take some time to develop a good bond with your friend and if you are lucky it can happen within days it all depends on the breed of rabbit you have.

Showing her that you don't want to hurt her and that you mean well will be the most rewarding experience. Act in a relaxed manner and let the bonding come naturally. If you show any sign of anxiousness, you will impart the sense to the rabbit which can impede the familiarization process. If a rabbit has had a bad experience with humans in the past, it is likely to take more time to adapt to her new environments and owners, but with love and gentle care, it should eventually become a happy, well-adjusted pet.

Take your time and let the rabbit come to you on her own terms they are naturally curious. They love exploration. Therefore, if you are quiet and patient she will come over to study you. Try not to pet her right away as she may be hesitant to trust you, at first sight, rabbits generally dislike being held. As she comes to you allow her to explore and have the assurance that you are not a threat. Once she is assured that you are not a threat she becomes relaxed and receptive to your tutoring. This is a crucial step for a strong and healthy relationship. If you allow her to dictate the tempo you will reduce her fear significantly. They become more affectionate when they feel completely comfortable and secure in your company.

Food can easily win a rabbit heart; give a few small treats at the time you are getting to know each other. Eating together builds trust. Treats are a very effective way of getting your bunny to trust you. They love you more as you give them food. Let the rabbit realize that getting closer to you will always bring a rewarding experience. Using small amounts of food at first and trying again a few more times, petting gently and then removing your hand.

Repeat the exercise and gradually increase the amount of interaction. As you do this over and over, the rabbit will get comfortable with you and associate your presence with good things and start to trust you with interaction.

You've got to get on the same level as your rabbit while developing the relationship. They are small and can only view your feet and legs. You have to sit or lie down on the floor to get to their level. When you are at the same level the threat factor subsides and the rabbit will want to know more about you. Gradually she becomes comfortable with your presence and scent which opens up the way for a closer relationship. They seem to enjoy listening to humans in a calm and composed voice, so try to speak softly and gently to win over your new friend. You can talk to them when they are walking about or in their cages. Whichever talk gently and don't shout to scare them.

Playing with your rabbit strengthens the bond between you. Rabbits are social animals; they want to have fun and exercise. Playtime with you will not only give them fun and exercise, but it also helps you to understand them better and stimulates them mentally as well.

Before the playtime begins, you need to spend some time observing your new friend. Watch for any signs that can make her uncomfortable with a game. Know her likes and dislikes. This is important for you to choose appropriate activities that the two of you can enjoy together. And if you suspect your rabbit is struggling to cope with the exercise, you should stop or try a different game.

Things you should never do while bonding with your rabbit

Here are some things you need to avoid while developing a bond with your rabbit. They can create set back to any progress you have made and make it hard to get your relationship to the point you envisage. You may need to start over again.

Do not force affection. Let the process be determined by the rabbit. You can only prompt but don't enforce it. Let the rabbits come to you when they feel comfortable.

· Don't rake them by surprise: Taking them by surprise will only scare them and put them in panic mode.

· Do not try to touch their face, nose or chin when they show signs of nervousness as they can bite you.

· If you want to lift them or remove them from their cage and you observe that they are too nervous, you have to wait until they have calmed down. Provide a treat if it is helpful.

· Do not carry them without having a solid grip because they may try to scramble away and become angry or disturbed.

· Do not chase, yell or play in a way where it seems you are aggressive. This is dangerous the rabbit will think you are a predator and lose trust in you quickly.

Rabbit's vocalizations and body language can tell you a lot about the mood and feeling of the rabbit. In developing a bond you have to consider this. When you learn to observe their body language and listen to their vocalization you will build up a sound relationship with your little friend. You will read more about this in the next chapter of this book.

9 How to Protect Rabbits from Predators

The safety of your pet from predators should be a big concern if your house rabbit stays outdoors in your garden. Many wild animals hunt rabbits. While the practice is most common in the wild, but some predators live and hunt in towns and cities, too. After providing protection from the weather elements the next thing is provision for safety from predators. It is not uncommon for some pet animals to attack your rabbits. You have to be vigilant if you keep other pets such as cats and dogs. They could be a threat to your bunny unless you have taken time to bond them.

The good thing is that you can protect your pet. These predators are opportunist who will seize any chance to attack an unprotected rabbit. Some attack at night, while others are active in the day time.

Depending on the area you live, the specific predators in your place may vary but the most common rabbit predators include:

- Dogs and wolves. They can attack at any time.
- Cats, including pet cats and bobcats. They can attack your rabbit at night or during the day.
- Birds of prey, such as hawks, eagles, falcons, and owls. They can attack your rabbit at night or during the day. Some are active in the day while some in the night.
- Large snakes. Depending on the species, they may attack at any time of day.
- Coyotes. Can attack at any time.
- Raccoons and Badgers. They are naturally nocturnal and will attack at night.
- Foxes. They can attack at night and sleep in the daytime.

Wild rabbits rely on their speed to escape predators but our pet rabbits living in an enclosed area (hutch or cage) depend majorly on you as a pet owner to be saved from predators. They are vulnerable- there's nowhere for them to run when a predator appears. You need to take good measures against threats from predators and ensure that your rabbit is protected from them. Here are some safety measures.

Keeping your Rabbit Indoors

If predation is a big concern in your area the most effective way to protect your rabbits is to house them indoors. They 'll be happy and get well living inside homes as long as they have access to food, water, toys and enough space to play, You can let them outside under your supervision in a covered run if you so wish. But never let them outside unsupervised. Your presence can scare some predators. Predators such as foxes are usually scared of humans, and won't venture near if you're around. Furthermore, some rabbits are escapee artists they can exploit any holes or gaps in fencing and escape the yard.

Predator-Proof Your Rabbit's Cage or Hutch

If you can't keep your rabbit indoors you have to Predator-Proof Your Rabbit's living area to deter predators. Make their cage strong and sturdy to secure your rabbit and prevent penetration from predators. Some predators can fly, and others can dig.

They can exploit any loophole to attack your pet. So you'll need to make sure that the cage is impenetrable from the side, above, and underneath.

To protect your rabbits from hawks and other predators that hunt from above, install a roof over your rabbit's run or exercise pen. This can be made of wood paneling or a sturdy wire mesh.

Make Your Yard Unattractive to Predators

The long-term solution for protecting your rabbit from these unwanted visitors is to try all possible means to prevent them from gaining access to your yard. Make your yard unattractive to them by keeping the area clean and free from places they can hide to lunch attack. Keep your yard tidy, cut trees and tall grasses that can harbor them. Cover or eliminate any nearby open water that might attract animals to drink. Keep tight lids on trash cans. And make your yard free of food scraps. Do your best to ensure that they don't venture near your yard, it is possible for rabbits to become so frightened and die of shock they often freeze when confronted by a predator. Although it's uncommon, it can happen.

Bond your rabbit with other pets

Other pets such as dogs and cats are animals of prey and will ordinarily kill rabbits. Although not all will instinctively kill them but most will. Never allow your untrained dog and cat near your rabbit without your supervision. The good thing is that they can be trained to live together.

Part Three: Common Rabbit Diseases.

This section contains rabbit general health information and an overview of their most common health problems. The information provided here is not meant to substitute for competent veterinary care. It is provided to educate pet rabbit owners to identify signs of illness in their pet rabbits, and in emergencies, know what to do to save the situation. Whenever in doubt, you should always consult a rabbit-savvy vet immediately who will be able to discover underlying health problems upon examination.

We first take a look at how to prevent diseases and then discuss about clinical signs you might notice in your sick rabbit and some of the conditions and diseases that are associated with the symptoms. The next chapter takes a look at specific health issues.

10 Preventing Diseases in Rabbits

Rabbit's health can deteriorate fast if they are not eating, drinking, pooping or peeing normally. It will be a great help if you as a pet owner have a good knowledge of what a healthy rabbit requires and the subtle signs that can tell you your rabbit is ill. The good thing is that some of these problems can be prevented before they become life-threatening issues. Often there are subtle changes in your rabbit's behavior that may be an indication of a disease process occurring. The earlier these problems are detected and prevented the better the chance of your rabbit living a healthy life. Good care and close observations will help you detect the early signs of problems, and prevent diseases developing.

The best way to stop your rabbit health issues is to prevent them from happening. An occasional vet visit is a good idea, but you should also check out your pet rabbit regularly at home by handling and examining her. Doing the following exercise regularly will prepare you for any first aid emergencies that may arise and help your rabbit to live a much healthier life.

Nose: Check that the rabbit nose is dry and clean and listen for normal, regular breathing.

Mouth: Check that your rabbit's teeth are not overgrown or broken.

Fur: Feel your rabbit's body for unusual lumps, cuts or bruises.

Toes: Ensure that her toes are all straight, with no signs of infection.

Nails: Check that her nails aren't too long. Too long nails can become infected or tear-off and bleed when knocking on things accidentally.

Genital area: Check the genital area and ensure that it is clean and dry.

Urine: Check her urine for unusual color, odor, or consistency. Sudden changes in urination habits may be a sign of **infection**.

Droppings: Check your bunnies droppings for any abnormality

First-aid Kit

Having a first aid kit can be a great way to deal with some minor medical issues that calls for attention. Here is a list of a few items **for your rabbit first aid kit.**

A heating pad or hot water bottle- To treat shock or hypothermia

Baby Food- When a sick rabbit won't eat, baby food comes in handy to feed your bunny. Look for pure pumpkin or squash with no preservatives and give with a syringe to help keep her strength up.

Cotton-tipped swabs— Used mainly for applying some medications and also for cleaning rabbit's ears

*Electrolyte powder—*Electrolyte powder comes in handy for a rabbit that is suffering from severe diarrhea. Add the powder to the water of a sick rabbit.

Gauze Pads, Cotton Balls, Q-tips & tweezers-To clean & bandage wounds and cleaning ears/eyes

Hydrogen- Hydrogen peroxide is used to wash down wounds and remove debris.

Mineral Oil- This is used for the treating ear mite's infection, a cotton swab dipped in mineral oil can be used to gently clean the ear.

Nail Clippers- Use to trim nails and overgrown teeth

Neomycin Ophthalmic- Use to treat eye infections/conjunctivitis

Non-latex gloves and/or hand sanitizer- To prevent the spread of germs between you & your rabbit

Plastic syringes— Having several plastic syringes on hand is a good idea. They are used to administer oral medication or food/water if your bunny won't eat.

Saline- To gently wash eye area with a sterile gauze pad

Scissors - To cut things; get ones with rounded tips

Stethoscope - (for listening to your rabbit intestinal sounds and the heart and lungs to watch out for any issue)

Styptic powder- This comes in handy for bleeding nails

Thermometer – This is needed to monitor your rabbit temperature. The normal body temperature of a healthy rabbit should be between 101-103 degrees Fahrenheit

Towels— A good number of absorbent cotton towels are useful for wrapping heat pads and help hold rabbits during treatment.

Tweezers- This comes in handy in removing bot flies, maggots, debris.

Vinegar: Use to wash down rabbit cages as a mild sterilizer.

One other most important addition to your first aid kit is the phone number of your local veterinarian. Tape it to the first aid box so you don't have to search for it in an emergency.

11 Symptoms of Sickness

A rabbit that is fed correctly, kept clean and given sufficient care is usually healthy. However, rabbits are susceptible to some diseases. Knowing about symptoms of common illnesses will help you about what to do to handle the situation. You will be able to recognize when to call for the attention of a vet. Usually, most of these signs are an indication of abnormal health conditions. Taking appropriate action can save the situation for you and your rabbit. Here are some clinical signs that will manifest when a rabbit is suffering from any type of disease.

Abscesses- An abscess is a pocket of fluid and pus caused by a bacterial infection. Rabbit abscesses are normally found in soft tissue or in the bone where there has been an injury. It can also occur in the jawline because of dental problems. To give your rabbit the best possible chance of recovery you need to get her to your vet as quickly as you can.

Anorexia—Loss of appetite- Loss of appetite can occur gradually or unexpectedly. It can lead to a lack of gut movements which in turn can result in the onset of shock due to bacterial poisons. The condition may well be associated with abdominal pain or swelling, passing mucus instead of droppings. If your rabbit fails to eat for more than four to six hours you should consult your vet.

Bloat - Bloat is a condition that can come suddenly; it is caused by the presence of bad bacteria that builds up in the intestines as a result of incorrect diet. The development releases excess gas into the stomach of the rabbit and causes it to get strained. It makes a healthy rabbit to suddenly stop eating and defecating. Affected rabbit may appear very tired, eyes appear to be sunken in, and hair will look rough and lifeless. Bloat can be fatal and dangerous to your rabbit. You should seek veterinary help when you suspect your rabbit is having the problem. Bloat can be prevented by ***giving your pet rabbit*** high-fiber hay regularly. Do not switch brands of feed or introduce any new foods or treats for baby rabbits that are less than 14wks old. Also try not to expose the rabbit to any forms of stress-inducing situations – such as loud noises, changing cages, and long journeys.

Blood in the urine- This is often a symptom of urolithiasis.

 Change in Urine Color or Cloudiness- The color of rabbit urine comes from plant pigments in the food or from normal pigments produced in the wall of the bladder. The normal urine color of rabbit urine can range from yellow to dark orange-red. Any change in appearance is a sign of infection. Your bunny can develop a disease of the bladder or kidneys and may show abnormalities such as blood in the urine, straining to urinate, frequent urination, or the complete inability to urinate.

Constipation- Constipation is a condition that arises when your rabbit is producing little or no dropping at all. It may be that there are hard faeces which are difficult for the rabbit to expel. Constipation can be a symptom of serious health problems such as acute bloat, broken back, ileus, volvulus, or other obstruction of the intestinal tract. It should be treated immediately.

Convulsions—Rabbits suffering from problems such as toxoplasmosis, RHD, and heat prostration may go into convulsions.

Dermatitis— This is skin inflammation which can be caused by infestations of ear mites, fur mites, scabies or fleas. Dermatitis may lead to hair loss or reddened, swollen, skin for the rabbit.

Diarrhea- Rabbits produce two types of droppings: feces and cecotropes. The feces appear solid while the cecotropes look soft and watery. Diarrhea occurs when both dropping are watery. It can be caused by incorrect diet, stress or cold and can be a consequence of another illness. It is a life-threatening issue that calls for urgent attention. Take your rabbit to the vet immediately you suspect diarrhea infection. The good thing is most **rabbit's** diarrhea cases can be easily prevented **with** dietary modification. Give your pet a little extra care; keep her environment clean, dry, quiet, and stress-free.

Difficulty breathing— This usually happens to rabbits suffering from respiratory diseases which include, flared nostrils when breathing, snuffles, pneumonia, RHD, and heat stress.

Drooling-This is a sign of dental disease in rabbits. It is a condition that causes a rabbit's teeth to be worn down improperly or poor alignment.

Failure to control urine release-This may be a symptom of a broken back, toxoplasmosis or bladder infection.

Lack of coordination- This may be a symptom of spinal injury or injury to the limbs, poisoning, enterotoxemia, heat exhaustion and arthritis.

Loss of balance or head tilt-Head tilt is a condition often caused by bacterial infections of the middle and inner ear or the brain. An affected rabbit may struggle to stand up and her head may circle always in one direction. It is a dangerous disease that can get transmitted to other rabbits or humans. Therefore, it should be treated immediately.

Low body temperature — a healthy rabbit has a body temperature of 100-140F. Low body temperature can be a symptom of acute bloat, ileus, mucoid enteropathy, and mycotoxicosis.

Malformed fecal pellets- It may be as a result of gastrointestinal stasis infection.

Nasal discharge— Discharge from the nose may be a symptom of snuffles, heat stress or rabbit pox.

Obesity- Obesity or overweight is as much a problem in house rabbits as it is in any other species.it is mainly caused in rabbits by incorrect feeding. Diets that is too high in dry food as contained in commercial rabbit diet and too low in hay. Overweight plays a key part in the health of a rabbit and is considered a pet welfare issue. Affected rabbits are not able to function properly because of their large size and excessive body fat. Obesity is common among middle-aged rabbits that are housed in a confined area such as cages; it can affect both male and female rabbits.

An obsessed rabbit can be identified with a physical examination. A typically overweight rabbit tends to be more than 20 to 40 percent of the normal weight. The fat usually covers the ribs under its layer and skin. Other signs of obesity may include difficulty breathing and excessively tiredness.

Ocular discharge— Ocular discharge may be caused by the presence of dust or a foreign object in the eye of the rabbit. It can also be a result of bacterial infection of the eye.

Pain— Rabbit body pain can be a symptom of several diseases and conditions, including acute bloat, volvulus, and mycotoxicosis.

Paralysis—Paralysis can be a consequence of severe malnutrition or fracture of the spine. It can also be as a result several diseases including arthritis, mycotoxicosis and, encephalitozoonosis.

Scratching—Excessive body scratching can be as a result of infection from ear mites, fur mites, scabies, fleas, or ringworm.

Sneezing or coughing —Sneezing is a sign of respiratory disease which include nasal discharge, flared nostrils when breathing, snuffle, stretched necks and open mouth breathing. It may be caused by dust, fumes, or allergies.

12 Common Rabbit Diseases

The diseases included in this chapter are some of the common diseases the rabbit owner would be most likely to encounter. **They ar**e by no means all that might be found in pet rabbits. Please do not rely solely upon the information provided in this chapter for a definitive diagnosis of what might be troubling your rabbit. Your veterinarian will be in the best position to do the correct analysis.

Acute Bloat *(tympany)*

Cause: An incorrect diet which leads to gas accumulation in the abdomen. .
Symptoms: loss of appetite, enlarged abdomen, failure to defecate, hair looking rough and lifeless.
Prevention: Proper feeding.

Gastrointestinal stasis; GI (or gut)

Cause: This include improper feeding (high starch and low fiber), causing the digestive system to slow down or stop working completely. Other causes include stress or lack of exercise.

Symptoms: Malformed fecal pellets, loss of appetite and tiredness.

Prevention: Diet and exercise. Make sure your rabbit is feeding properly. Your rabbit should have a good high-fiber diet See part two of this book to learn more on how to feed your rabbit for a healthy living. Let them have regular exercise.

Skin parasites (ectoparasites)

Parasite infection is common with rabbits in the wild. But pet rabbit too can be infected. Parasites like fleas, warble flies, worms and protozoans may attack your pet rabbits.

Fleas

A flea is a tiny creature that feeds off mammalian blood.

Causes: By contact with infected animals such as domestic dog or cat

Symptoms: Frequent scratching, flea dirt visible. Presence of tiny brown droppings in the rabbit fur

Prevention: Reduce your rabbit's exposure to fleas. Take great care to keep your pet in a clean, safe environment. Make sure and that they are groomed regularly, don't allow contact with other animals in the household especially those allowed outside, they can easily infect your rabbit with fleas. Watch your rabbit closely for signs of infestation and treat it immediately.

Ear mite

Causal agent: The parasite *Psoroptes cuniculiis*

Symptoms: Itching around the ear, head, and neck of the rabbit, dry and scaly skin, and hair loss in affected areas.

Prevention: Ear mite infestation is highly contagious. Maintain a clean, safe environment for your rabbit. Always have any new rabbit checked for ear mites whether signs of infestation are present or not.

Scabies *(Mange)*

Causal agent: *Sarcoptes scabei* or *Notoedres cati.*

Symptoms: Frequent scratching, loss of hair (particularly on face area)

Transmission: Direct contact.

Prevention: Scabies is contagious, so keep your rabbits from affected animals.

Internal parasites

Cocci

Causal Agent: microscopic parasites that live in the intestine of the rabbit.

Symptoms: Usually mild or no noticeable symptoms. But in severe cases-diarrhea, poor appetite, mucous in feces, weight loss, and sometimes death can occur.

Transmission: Rabbits that recover from the infection can become carriers. Intake of contaminated food or water by the rabbit.

Prevention: Good management practices that reduce the danger of fecal contamination of feed, water, and hutch floors. Also, it is a disease that affects other house animals, such as chicken and dogs. Early detection and prevention are crucial to the wellbeing of your rabbit.

Roundworms (ascarius)

Causal agent: *Baylisascaris procyonis.*

Symptoms: This depends on the degree of infestation. Light infestations produce a little effect; heavy infestation may cause diarrhea head tilt, tremors, lethargy, paralysis, and even death.

Transmission: Ingestion of contaminated feed and bedding.

Prevention: Good management and proper sanitation.

Pinworm

Causal agent: *Passalurus ambiguus* (a nematode).

Symptoms: Glistening, white, and 1/2 inch long worms visible in fresh feces, excessive grooming of anal area.

Transmission: Through ingestion of feed and water contaminated by the droppings of infected animals.

Prevention: Proper sanitation can minimize the effect.

Tapeworm

Causal agent: Cittotaenia ctenoides: flat, ribbon-shaped, and made up of numerous segments

Symptoms: Anorexia, enlarged abdomen, swellings under skin.

Transmission: Through ingestion of feed and water containing tapeworm segments and eggs from the droppings of dogs.

Prevention: Good sanitation and proper management. Don't allow your rabbits to eat grass in areas where dogs run.

Bacteria Diseases

A bacterial infection is common in pet rabbits causing a variety of diseases and symptoms. This section focuses on the more common bacterial and diseases.

Pasteurellosis

Causesal agent: *Pasteurella multocida.*

Symptoms: Clinical manifestations of pasteurellosis in rabbits include but are not limited to abscesses, weepy eye, snuffles, pneumonia, reproductive tract infections, torticollis, and septicemia.

Transmission: Direct contact. Rabbits that have runny noses and sneezing are most likely to spread the bacteria. Acute infections of the disease are highly contagious, chronic infections are less contagious.

Prevention: Improper feeding, stress, dust, and high ammonia levels may make a bunny more susceptible. The best preventive measure is to reduce stress and practice good sanitation.

Pneumonia

Causes: Inadequate ventilation, sanitation, and nesting material are predisposing factors causing acute inflammation in the lungs of the rabbit leading to dysfunction of the entire respiratory system.

Symptoms: Some common signs include: difficulty breathing, nose discharge, weight loss, eye discharge, fever or sneezing.

Transmission: direct contact.

Prevention: Good sanitation and proper ventilation.

Salmonellosis

Causal agent: *Salmonella enteritidis, S. typhimurium.*

Symptoms: Fever and occasionally diarrhea and there may be no symptoms but sudden death.

Transmission: direct contact or ingestion of feed contaminated with poultry or rodent feces.

Prevention: Good management. Keep away any feed or bedding contaminated by birds or rodents.

Snuffles

Causal agent: Pasteurella *multocida.*

Symptoms: It causes discharge, redness, squinting in the eyes and sneezing. Others include sticky yellowish discharge from the nose, snuffling, sneezing, coughing, lethargy, depression, wry neck (head tilt).

Transmission: Close contact with an infected rabbit can easily transfer the disease to your rabbit.

Prevention: Good sanitation. Reducing stress for infected rabbits is a good way of saving the situation.

Treponematosis *(vent disease, syphilis, spirochetosis)*

Causes: *Treponemia papaluiscuniculi.* It is seen in both sexes

Symptoms: Small vesicles or ulcers are formed, which eventually become covered with a heavy scab. Rabbits may also develop ulcers on the ears, lips, eyelids, and face.

Transmission: By breeding, from the doe to offspring. Venereal contact.

Prevention: Infected rabbits should not be used for breeding.

Viral Disease

The viral disease is not common with the pet rabbit. (RHD and myxomatosis) are perhaps the most terrible virus diseases that can affect a pet rabbit. When it occurs it may affect the integument, gastrointestinal tract or, central nervous system.

Rabbit Viral Hemorrhagic Disease

Causal agent: calicivirus that affects only rabbits of the *Oryctolagus cuniculus sp*

Symptoms: Loss of appetite, lethargy, fever, bleeding from the nose, mouth, and rectum is sometimes seen and even sudden death.

Transmission: It is a *highly* contagious disease, and will rapidly infect all the rabbits. Contact of healthy rabbits with an infected rabbit or the feces, fur of an infected rabbit.

Prevention: Good management. Always wash hands thoroughly before handling your rabbits when coming indoors, particularly when coming from an area where there is an outbreak.

Myxomatosis

Causal Agent: myxoma virus, a member of the poxvirus group.

Symptoms: conjunctivitis that rapidly becomes more marked and is accompanied by a milky ocular discharge, other signs include lethargy, anorexia, rough coat, fever, labored breathing, swelling of genitals, lips, eyelids, and nose.

Transmission: It is spread by biting insects which including fleas and mosquitoes or by close contact between an infected rabbit and a susceptible rabbit.

Prevention: Vaccination is a good preventive measure against the disease.

Gastrointestinal Condition

Gastrointestinal infection is a common problem with pet rabbits. It is probably one of the most serious, immediate problems your pet rabbit can have. This is because rabbits' digestive systems are susceptible to being upset. The good thing is that most of the problems are relatively easy to treat with good pet management.

Other Conditions

Bladder Stones

Bladder or calcium stones can occur when the rabbit finds it difficult processing calcium through its kidneys correctly. Sign of infection includes the following; straining to urinate, wetness around the genital area, semi-solid (like toothpaste) urine, or blood in the urine and inability to keep to litter box habits. Calcium stone is easy to control at the early stage before it becomes a life-threatening situation. Take your pet for a veterinary visit when you detect any of the signs mentioned above before it causes any permanent damage to your rabbit's health or life-span.

Heat Stroke

Heatstroke or heat exhaustion can be very dangerous to your pet rabbits. Rabbits are more prone to heatstroke than humans. It occurs when they are exposed to high temperatures, even for a short period. Signs of **heat stroke** include the following; unresponsiveness, being uncoordinated and convulsions.

Enteritis

Enteritis is one of the most common disease conditions in rabbits. It is an inflammation of the intestine caused by a sudden change in the rabbit's diet. It is commonly seen at weaning which means; it mainly affects baby rabbits between 5 and 8 weeks old when they are weaned from their mother's milk to other food. The risk of enteritis in your rabbit can be minimized by making gradual dietary changes and ensuring that baby rabbits have regular access to fresh clean water, hay, and fresh vegetables. Also, avoid starting newly weaned kits on a news feed.

Book 2; Guinea Pigs

The Essential Guide to Ownership, Care, and Training for Beginners

Dave Josephson

About this Book

Guinea pigs are sweet-tempered, expressive, and cheerful pets. They are inexpensive and pretty easy to care for, compared to a lot of pets. However, they do require care and certain supplies to keep them healthy and comfortable. To enjoy their love and affection you must first give them the necessary care and attention they deserve. This book shares all the basic information you need to know to successfully own a pet guinea pig. It is an extensive care guide for first-time owners who wants details about guinea pig care.

1 Reasons Guinea Pigs Make Wonderful Pets

Guinea pigs are very bright creatures. **They make great pets for people limited by space but love social and affectionate companion.** They're sweet, expressive, and cheerful. Compared to a lot of pets, they are pretty easy to care for. **Their** docile nature and cute appearance make them **favorite pets to many people. Even though originated from a tropical area they can adapt well to cooler climates.** They can be kept outdoors or indoors **with minimal requirements.** So if you desire a pet that is small, charming and affectionate then a guinea pig is the ideal choice for you. They make good pets for adults and children alike.

Here are some reasons why pet guinea pigs are good for you.

Low maintenance

Guinea pigs are inexpensive pets. They are usually either free to adopt or cost less at pet stores. Also, they do make great pets for small apartment owners– they only need a little room compared to other pets. **Guinea pigs** are very easy to feed, **they are vegans;** they consume a mix of pellets, hay and fresh produce. They don't eat animal products of any kind -meat or dairy. Guinea pigs are an ideal pet for busy individuals who have unpredictable schedules; they are relatively easy to care for.

They Are Clean

Guinea pigs are clean animals and can be potty-trained, even though they have a small bladder. They might even get sick if they are kept in dirty environments. A guinea pig usually grooms itself but would appreciate occasional brushing with a soft-bristled brush. If kept in a clean environment, they produce little to no odor.

They Are Quiet

Guinea pigs are quiet. They do not make loud noises or shrieks to disturb their owners. They may scream and whistle when they want your attention, but these noises are not bothersome.

They are Friendly

Guinea pigs have a good temperament. They are social and intelligent creatures that can form emotional bonds with their owners. They are endearing pets who love to have companions in their homes and love to be held. They can also be taught tricks. Guinea pigs are sweet-tempered and not destructive.

Guinea pigs are Entertaining

If you want a pet with a personality that you can play with, then you should consider getting a guinea pig. Guinea pigs are colorful and entertaining. They will jump up and down, squeak, and squeal. They love the mental stimulation provided by play opportunities.

Guinea Pigs are Great pet for Children

Guinea pigs make a great pet for children; they are less fragile than rabbits and not as skittish as smaller rodents. Guinea pigs have a friendly disposition and would respond to lots of cuddles from children. Getting a pet for a child has lots of benefits; it makes them responsible and helps them to learn how to care for the needs of another living thing.

2 Guinea Pigs Facts

Origin

Despite their name guinea pigs are not related to pigs , but rather rodents and they are not from Guinea. They originated from the Andes, in Peru and Bolivia, where they were originally being kept mainly for food.

The scientific name of the guinea pig is *Cavia porcellus*. They belong to the family Caviidae, which is a family of South American rodents. Their nickname is "cavy," which is possibly derived from their scientific name Cavia.

Gender

A male guinea pig is called a *boar* **and a female is called a** *sow* and a young one is called a pup.

Baby pups are born ready for the world. They are born with their eyes open and body covered in fur. They can drink from a water bottle and can eat hay within hours of being born.

Socialization

They crave the company of others of their kind and will do well in pairs or small groups. Breeding **will increase their number, so keeping single-sex groups (or neutered and spayed pets) are advisable.**

It is best to introduce the guinea pigs to each other when they are young, to encourage bonding, but adults can also bond given the necessary training.

If a sow is uninterested in a boar during courtship, she will sometimes squirt a jet of urine at the persistent boar.

Guinea pigs are herd animals. **In the wild, they live in 'herds' with a dominant male who breeds with the females.** They always march in single file, with the biggest guinea pig at the front and the young protected in the middle.

Category

Generally, there are two categories of guinea pigs: long-haired and short-haired. Short-haired guinea pigs are typically easier to care for than long-haired ones.

Fitness

Guinea pigs are unable to make their own vitamin C like humans. They need to get it from their diet.

Their teeth are constantly growing like rabbits so they need chewing on the high fiber of grass hay to keep their teeth worn down. Also, they have **continuously growing nails that need to be trimmed regularly.**

Desexing your Guinea Pig is a good idea. It reduces the chances of contacting some serious diseases and ensures a calm temperament.

 A female guinea pig should give birth before 6 months of age. After this age, she is likely to face a difficult pregnancy if bred. **The reason is that**

the pelvic bones become fused which can prevent her from smooth delivery.

Guinea pigs naturally run a higher temperature of about 101° F. This high temperature places them at increased risk during hot weather.

Guinea pigs produce two kinds of poos: normal and cecotropes. Cecotropes are rare to see because guinea pigs eat them directly from their cecum, in a process known as coprophagy.

Abilities

Guinea pigs are incredibly sensitive to loud noises. And have good hearing which is more sensitive than human hearing. They are highly sensitive to the predator's presence.

They have poor eyesight. Their vision isn't too good, with poor depth perception.

They are not good at climbing but they can run very quickly. They are very intelligent and can even be taught to use a litter box or do tricks.

Guinea pigs typically live for about 5 or 6 years, though they may live up to 9. This varies by individual, quality of care, and environment.

3 Guinea Pig Housing Plan

Despite their small size, guinea pigs need lots of space to run around and exercise. Their housing must have a separate sleeping area and a haven where they can retreat to when they feel afraid or need some peace. So, when choosing guinea pig hutches, you should consider the size, the spacious the better. Housing them in a blissfully spacious environment will contribute greatly to their health and well-being.

Here are general guidelines for guinea pig hutches

The housing size depends on how many guinea pigs you have. A minimum of 7.5 square feet cage is recommended for one guinea pig, but more is better if you have space. For two guinea pigs, a minimum of 7.5 square feet is equally good but 10.5 square feet is preferred.

Location

Once you have the housing ready the next important thing to consider is the location. A guinea pig can be kept indoors or outdoors but you need to ensure you create the right environment for them wherever you decide to choose. Housing them indoors will help them get sufficient attention and have more human interaction.

Temperature: The normal temperature range for guinea pigs is approximately 65-75 degrees Fahrenheit. Their cage should not be located near strong heat sources such as wood stoves, fireplaces, and radiator. Guinea pigs do not sweat when they become too warm and are most vulnerable to heatstroke. Also, it should not be placed by a large window where they will get excessive heat from the sun in summer or a draft in winter months.

They should not be kept outdoors if the temperature falls below 60 degrees F. They don't do well under humid conditions. Humidity promotes the growth of mold in their hay and bedding and can make them more susceptible to infection. Therefore, choose a draft-free area and place the cage on an elevated surface.

If you plan to keep them outdoors, you will need a solid and sturdy spacious hutch to prevent predator attack. They are vulnerable to predators. Also, make sure their cage is safe from other pets who may see them as prey.

Guinea pigs can be prone to stress, so the hutch should be placed in an area where there isn't a lot of noise or traffic. A family room or living room or a place that's visited regularly but that doesn't have constant traffic will be an ideal place. They enjoy being near family activity and cherish interaction from their caregivers. Whatever be the case make sure your pet has a place to retreat if they need some quietness.

Once you have the right cage space and location for your guinea pig, your next goal is to make sure it feels like a home.

Cage Supplies

The bedding

The bedding should not be made out of anything fluffy, as this can be harmful to them if ingested. Straw and softwood products such as pine and cedar shavings can also be dangerous to the guinea pig's health. They are poisonous to them and can actually cause serious problems with their respiratory systems. Straw doesn't absorb droppings at all which makes keeping a clean environment a bit difficult. The best bedding for guinea pigs is timothy hay, which provides the main component of their food. If you decide to go with this option, make sure to train them to not eat their bedding hay by providing a hayrack with pellets mixed. Also, try to change out the hay often so that they don't consume soiled hay. You need to provide extra bedding in the winter months to keep them warm.

Water bowls, dishes, and bottles: You need these supplies for eating and drinking. If your guinea pig is not drinking from water bottles you can use the bowls. The bowl should be heavy and kept off the ground to prevent your guinea pigs from fouling in them. Make sure they are cleaned regularly and refill their water once a day.

Toys: The guinea pigs will enjoy having toys that they can chew as well as places to hide in the hutch. They can easily get bored or depressed if they don't have enough to do. Always make sure these toys are safe. You should avoid plastic toys, as these can be harmful if ingested as guinea pigs enjoy gnawing and chewing. Purchase chew toys specifically designed for guinea pigs. They are available in pet shops and online.

Other Recommendations

Do not use a cage with wire flooring, as it can be somewhat uncomfortable for your guinea pigs and difficult for cleaning. Also, they have tiny and delicate legs that can easily get caught in wire or mesh. This could lead to severe injury, loss of a limb or even death. Make sure that the flooring is smooth without nails, ridges and not meshed. A cage with a bottom tray will be a good option. This will make things a bit easier for you as you can easily slide it out to swap out bedding.

Outdoor run

It is important to make provision for a run. The run should provide enough space for your guinea pig to get fresh air, sufficient exercise and to graze. Ensure that the run is in a safe and shaded area with sufficient grass for them to eat and run around on. It should be made of sturdy mesh, at least 16 gauge or less. It should also have a roof, to prevent predators such as cats or foxes trying to get at your guinea pigs.

Cleaning the Cage or Hutch

You must keep a clean environment for your Guinea Pigs for their well-being. They need hygienic and fresh environment in which to thrive. Make sure any leftover fruit or vegetables are cleaned out on a daily basis. Remove any soiled or muddy hay and replace it with fresh hay. Also, the cage should be cleaned out at least once a week. (depending on the type of bedding you have and how quickly it becomes dirty).

4 Guide to Guinea Pig Breeds

Guinea pigs are available in so many different breeds. Each breed comes with its own distinctive features-color, size, and shape. Although they come in varieties, they mostly share similar behavior. Irrespective of the type of breed, they are adorable and offer great companionship to their owners.

Here is a list of some common breeds available. This will help you in making the choice of the pet that you would want in your home.

Short-haired guinea pig breed

The American

The American guinea pig originated in Peruvian Andes, South America. These breeds have a short, smooth coat and come in a wide range of colors. They're the popular breed of guinea pig, and their short coats make them relatively easy to keep in excellent condition. They do not require regular grooming. In addition to their delightful appearance, they also have a pleasant personality that makes them a great pet for families and any first-time pet owners. They can live for between 4 and 7 years and get along easily with other cavies.

.

The Himalayan guinea pig

The Himalayan guinea pigs are great breeds originated in South East Asia. They are considered as the Siamese cat among the breeds. They are usually born white with highlights of brown or black on their ears, feet, and nose. If exposed to too much sunlight or hot weather, the highlights may seem to disappear. They are mostly suitable for people who live in areas with not much heat. They can live for between 5 and 7 years.

White Crested Guinea Pigs

White Crested guinea pigs have smooth and short hairs which are easier to maintain. Their unique feature is the small patch of white hair in between their ears that looks like a small white crown above their head. They are cute and great crowd entertainers.

Rough coat Guinea pigs

Teddy guinea pigs

Teddy guinea pigs are born in many different colors. The texture and appearance of their hair make them popular. Their hairs stand all over their body giving them a springy coat that is dense, harsh, even and short which makes them look like a toy. They are an extraordinarily sweet-looking pet with a calm temperament. They can live for between 5 and 7 years.

The Rex

The Rex guinea pigs breeds originated in South America. They have a woolly texture rough coat. Their most distinctive feature is their huge droopy ears and broad head. Rex guinea pigs have a sweet temperament and loved to be held and pet. They can live up to 6 years.

The Abyssinian guinea pigs

The Abyssinian guinea pigs are among the oldest breeds of guinea pigs. Their distinctive feature is their hair formation which grows in rosettes outwards from their body. They come in lots of different colors and color arrangements, such as black and red, white and red, or grey. They are a good choice for first-time pet owners.

Long-haired Guinea Pigs

The Silkie

Silkie Guinea Pigs or sheltie guinea pig breed are known for their long, shiny and soft, smooth coat. They exist in a wide variety of different colors with .long, lustrous hair that can be some inches long. Among all the common guinea pig breeds, the Silkie is well-known for being the most gentle. Their unique hairstyle makes them charming and adorable pets. They can be high maintenance which makes them unsuitable choices for kids. Their average lifespan is 5 to 7 years.

The Peruvian guinea

The Peruvian guinea has long straight hair without any curl all over their bodies. These hairs sprout in multiple directions and can be grown to a reasonable length. They come in many different colors, from red to grey and to white and cream. They are highly intelligent and curious animals but keeping them takes extra effort. They appear more difficult to care when compared to other short-haired breeds as their wool can be high to maintain and require a lot of grooming. They are capable of growing to a maximum length of 24 inches and live up to 7 years.

Texel Guinea pig

Texel Guinea Pigs originated in France. They are known for their long, soft, thick hair that ends up on ringlets or curls all over their body, making them look a lot larger than their actual size. Texel guinea pigs come in a variety of different colors and make great show pets. Their fur needs a considerable amount of effort to maintain. They may not be an ideal pet option for kids or adults who could not spare time for regular maintenance and grooming. Their life span is between 4 and 7 years.

Coronet Guinea Pig

Coronet guinea pigs originated in England. They are very similar to Silkies, in that they have a very long, smooth coat that grows backward over the entire body which can even reach the ground. However, unlike the Silkie, the Coronet Guinea Pig has a rosette or coronet in the central of its head. They are curious, lively, and friendly. Like any other long-haired guinea pigs breeds, Coronets need frequent grooming. They can live up to 6 or 8 years.

Alpaca guinea pigs

Alpaca guinea pigs breed is quite similar to the Peruvian breed. They are considered by many guinea pig pet owners as among the most beautiful of all the breeds. They have a heavy textured coat that has multi colors on its ends as opposed to the its main body. They are friendly and adorable and do well mostly indoors. The alpaca guinea pig is moderately high maintenance guinea pigs compared to other species. Their hair requires brushing and de-tangling on a daily basis. Their lifespan is between 5 to 8 years.

Hairless Guinea Pigs

Some breeds of guinea pigs that are hairless. Some are completely hairless and some have a smattering of fur on their face and their feet. They are very susceptible to infection and would need special warm accommodation and a high energy diet.

The Baldwin guinea pig

The Baldwin guinea pig is completely bald. They are born with hair but after about two months their hair begins to fall out. Their skin is the same as the coat color. Baldwin is quite a strong species. They are not capable of dealing with really cold temperatures and so should be kept inside always. They cannot withstand any direct sunlight or severe weather and so they must be kept in the shade when you have them outside. They can live up to 6 years.

5 Guinea Pig Diet and Feeding Tips

Guinea pigs are natural herbivores, so they should be given a healthy, balanced diet. They do not require a particularly complicated diet, a nice combination of guinea pig hay, water, fresh vegetables, fresh fruit as well as a moderate amount of quality pellets, and a good source of vitamin C will make them happy. Providing adequate fiber in their diet is equally important for both their gastrointestinal system and general health.

The guinea pig digestive system is sensitive. If you need to change their diet, please make sure you introduce any new feed gradually over a few weeks. This is important to allow your guinea pigs' digestive systems to adjust, so they don't get sick. Blend any new food into the existing diet in small quantities and slowly increasing the amount.

Grass Hay

Grass hay is the most essential part of the diet of your guinea pigs. It provides the necessary fiber needed for good digestive health. It helps in wearing their teeth for good dental health. Guinea pigs' teeth grow continually through their life, they need to chew constantly to help keep them fill down. Grass hays should make up about 70%-80% of your guinea pig's diet.

The most common source of grass hay is timothy hay; other popular types are orchard grass hay and oat hay. Hay should be replaced often and store in a cool, dry place to allow air circulation, and don't give damp hay. Don't feed your guinea pig alfalfa or clover hay, as these are too high in protein and calcium.

Pellets

Pellets should mostly only contain a small portion of your cavy's diet. You should make use of pellets that are high in fiber and low in protein. It is good to use a pellet that is plain, with no extra seeds or tidbits, so that your cavy doesn't end up choosing the ones he likes and neglect the rest. Alfalfa hay-based is good for cavies less than a year, but if they are older than that, you should only give them pellets that are timothy hay-based.

Limit pellet intake as your guinea pig ages. Pellets with high protein content can lead to obesity and other health issues. Give fresh pellets always and only buy enough for a few months at a time. Store pellets in a closed container in a cool, dry place to avoid pellets becoming stale.

Fresh Vegetables and Fruits

Vegetables should be a good part of your guinea pig daily diet. Give them about one to two cups of fresh vegetables every day. Vegetables help balance out the nutritional needs in their diet. Feed fresh dark green vegies and be sure it is washed thoroughly before feeding them. Fruits are high in sugar and should be given in small quantities- no more than once a week as a full serving. Small, bite-sized portions served daily will delight your guinea pig and provide much-needed Vitamin C.

Suggested Healthy Vegetables

- Brussel Sprouts

- Carrots

- Cucumbers

- Endive

- Green capsicum

- Green Leaf Lettuce

- Radicchio

- Radish tops

- Raspberry leaves

Suggested Healthy Fruits

- Apples

- Blueberries

- Mangoes

- Melon

- Oranges and their appealing peels, too

- Papaya

- Pear

- Peach

- Pineapple

- Plum

- Raspberries and Strawberries

- Tomatoes

Cecotropes

Cecotropes are a necessary part of your guinea pig's diet. It is the natural way of supplementing the guinea pig's unique nutritional needs. They are small, soft pellets that contain nutrients absorbed from plants during the digestive process. They pass out through the anus from the large intestine of the guinea pig and are consumed immediately.

The Importance of Vitamin C

Guinea pigs have an increased risk of developing a Vitamin C deficiency. Unlike other rodents, they cannot produce their own vitamin C. It has to be given through their diet or with a supplement. To prevent scurvy and other health issues, they should be given 10 to 30 milligrams of Vitamin C every day. The best supplements are either chewable tablets or liquid vitamin C that can be taken using a syringe. You can provide vitamin C from natural sources, by supplementing with treats in the form of citrus fruits and vegetables. They should take daily Vitamin C rich foods such as leafy green veggies and capsicums (green, orange, and red). Other foods such as carrots, berries, pineapple, and kiwifruit, are also a good source of Vitamin C and a tasty treat for your guinea pigs but they should only be given sparingly because of their high sugar content.

Water

Water is an essential ingredient in guinea pig nutrition. Give them **fresh water** every day. Like any other animal, insufficient water intake can lead to dehydration. It can also make them develop urinary stones or crystals. Their water intake should be at least five ounces daily. Water bottles should be emptied, cleaned, and re-filled each day.

Foods to be avoided

It is imperative to know what not to feed your guinea pigs, as there are plenty of foods that might seem harmless but can, in fact, be detrimental to their health. They should not be given to your guinea pig, for various reasons. Some can be poisonous, some have no nutritional value, some can cause gas and some can cause bloat and some are too high in fat or sugar,

Some of the following foods should be avoided.

Salt licks or mineral blocks, animal byproducts, vegetables with a lot of calcium and iceberg lettuce and human foods such as pieces of bread, sugar, biscuits, sweets, dairy products, chocolate, pasta, crackers, or pickled foods.

Feed your guinea pig on a consistent schedule, preferably twice a day, morning and evening and don't overfeed. Guinea pigs have the tendency to overeat if given the chance. To prevent obesity, you have to regulate their eating pattern,. Remove uneaten pelleted feeds after about an hour and remove fresh fruits or vegetables that are left uneaten after 24 hours. Also, never add new food, including hay, before cleaning out the old food.

6 Understanding Your Pet Guinea Pig

Guinea pigs don't speak human language, but like all animals, they have their own unique language. They communicate with each other and with people using a wide variety of body postures and a few vocalizations. They have their own unique way of expressing different emotions such as anger, fear, happiness, or romance. They do make quite distinctive noises you might hear from them to call for your attention. Understanding what their behavior means will help you build a closer bond and care for them most effectively. It will also lead to personal satisfaction and enjoyment for both of you.

Guinea Pig Sounds

Here's a guide for some of the most common guinea pig sounds.

Wheeking: Wheeking sounds like a long and loud squeal or whistle and it is mostly used to communicate anticipation or excitement. Many guinea pigs will make a very loud noise in anticipation of getting some tasty treats at the sight of their owner with a food container.

Cooing: Cooing communicates reassurance in the guinea pigs world. It is a sound commonly used by sows to let their pups know that everything is okay and under control.

Purring: Guinea pigs do make purr sounds like cats. However, it has different meanings. The intensity of the sound and the accompanying body language determine the meaning oftentimes. A deep purring sound is an indication that your guinea pig is contented and comfortable at the moment. This is usually followed by a relaxed, calm posture. A higher-pitched purring sound, especially towards the end is likely a sound of annoyance. This is usually followed by tense and uneasiness. A shorter sounding, sometimes described as a "durr," may signify fear or uncertainty. This is usually accompanied by the guinea pig remaining motionless.

Teeth Chattering: Teeth chattering is a sign of an agitated or angry guinea pig. It is often accompanied by the guinea pig showing its teeth.

Hissing: Hissing is just like the hissing noise that a pet cat makes. It may also sound like chattering teeth and is a sign that your pet guinea pig is upset or aggressive.

Chirping: Chirping is perhaps the least understood sound that guinea pigs make. It is often made when your guinea pig is in a trance-like state. The meaning of this strange noise is not yet fully understood. It is a subject of much debate, with no firm conclusions.

Rumbling: A guinea pig rumble is similar to a purr, and the two guinea pig noises are often confused. However, the rumbling is deeper than a purring noise. The best way to distinguish them is by looking at the behaviors that accompanied them. Usually, the male guinea pigs rumble when he romances a female and sometimes females in season also make it.

Shrieking: This is a sound you hear from a distressed guinea pig. Shriek is indicative of physical pain, response to pain or immediate danger. It is a sound that should not be ignored. If your guinea pig makes this sound it is imperative to respond and investigate the cause immediately.

Whining: Whining is a way of showing disagreement. Although your guinea pigs do enjoy the company and being handled, sometimes they need their space. This high pitch noise is an indication that your guinea pig is no longer comfortable being handled, he wants to let go and roam free. It can also communicate annoyance or dislike for something another guinea pig is doing.

Reading Guinea Pig Body Language

Guinea pigs can also communicate through body language. Changes in their movements and posture can give clues about what is happening with them.

Freezing: This is a mode that signifies fear and doubt. A cavy that is frightened or uncertain about something in its immediate environment will freeze to the spot.

Sniffing: Guinea pigs like to sniff each other around the nose, chin, ears, and back end. They are doing this primarily to find out what is going on around them and to get to know others.

Touching Noses: Nose touching is a friendly greeting between guinea pigs.

Aggressive Actions: These can include raising their heads, hissing, rising on their hind ends with stiff legs, fidgeting, shuffling side to side on stiff legs, hair fluffing, and showing their teeth. If you notice these signs you should be on the alert, your guinea pig is scared or uncomfortable. Usually, you will hear hissing or teeth chattering sound accompanying these postures.

Licking: Most people consider this a sign of guinea pig affection.

Fidgeting While Being Held: This can often be a sign that your guinea pig doesn't want to be held at the moment or he needs to go to the bathroom.

Popcorning: popcorning is when your guinea pig hops straight up in the air, sometimes repeatedly high in the air. It signifies a state of extreme happiness and excitement in guinea pigs. It is commonly seen in young guinea pigs who are particularly joyful, pleased, excited or just feeling playful. Adult guinea pigs also popcorn, though they usually don't hop as high as younger ones.

7 How to Build a Stronger Bond with Your Guinea Pig

Guinea pigs are naturally shy and skittish so building a strong relationship in the early days with the family may not come easily. Depending on your cavy's personality, it may take a while for your new member to settle and adjust to its new environment. The initial stage requires some level of understanding and effort and commitment on your part. You have to make them comfortable as they tried to get used to their new environment and provide affection and positive reinforcement. Guinea pigs can become quite close to their favorite person, and be almost dog-like in terms of affection and behavior.

Remember that in order to properly bond with your guinea pig, it requires commitment. You should be prepared to spend reasonable time with them consistently every day. It is natural they get scared of you at first. It is important you give them time to adjust to your presence. Don't do anything that can scare or intimidate them. Guinea pigs are prey animal they have a strong flight freeze response. Before they can get proper bonding with you they need to overcome their natural instincts of fear. So you have to make the interaction between you and your guinea pig less stressful and frightening so that they can enjoy spending time with you.

Not all guinea pigs are created equal, and some may be shyer or friendlier than others. Many guinea pigs can take weeks, sometimes even months to get comfortable with the scents and sounds of their new owner or the environment. This just depends on each guinea pig's individual personality. A guinea pig with the previous experience of neglect and abuse will take much more effort to get to trust his human counterpart. Taking the time to properly bond with your pet will ensure a much better relationship. A well-bonded guinea pig is much more trainable and will learn new tricks significantly faster than one that is skittish. They will be a better pet, with a good quality of life.

Tips for Building a Stronger Bond with Your Guinea Pig

Give Your Guinea Pig Time to Adjust

After they have arrived at their new home it is important you give them time to get used to their surroundings. Avoid the temptation to pick up and hold your new guinea pigs immediately. You have to be patient to let the newest members of your family adjust and feel safe and comfortable in his new home. Be present and speak softly to give your pet the assurance that you are his friend indeed. Give your cavies some time to acclimate to their new environment. With time he won't be scared but this can take some weeks. Patience is the key.

Approach them gently

Your manner of approach can influence the bonding process. Guinea pigs are apprehensive and see anyone as a potential threat. Be careful not to make loud noises or sudden movements around their area. Jumping on them suddenly will make them stay in a state of caution. Approach them calmly and gently as you move near their habitat. Prepare their mind by speaking to them to let them know you are about to visit them. The less they are scared of you, the faster they will come to trust you.

Get a fellow Guinea pig

Guinea pigs are social animals; they enjoy the companionship of fellow guinea pigs. In the wild, they don't stay alone, they live in large herds. If you have one, consider adding one or two. This will give them the chance to form a bond with others and alleviate his anxiety about being alone.

Schedule Floor Time

Floor time is an excellent way to keep your guinea pig engaged in its environment. It can also be a great time for you to forge a strong bond with your pet. It should be a vital part of your daily guinea pig care schedule. Pick a set time each day, set up a safe floor area and try to include a place they can hide if they so wish. Engage your guinea with exercises; add toys, treats, set up mazes and obstacles with boxes and fabrics. Sit next to your cavy as he runs and explores his new world. Observe and get to know your little friend's personality.

Consistency

Guinea pigs are a creature of habitat. They are more comfortable with a routine. Strengthening the bond with them requires consistency. This is particularly vital if they are new to your home and unsure of their environments. Guinea pigs feel more secure and comfortable if they know what to expect. A consistent schedule eliminates the fear of not knowing what is going to happen next. Daily activities such as feeding, floor time, and pick-ups will make your guinea pig more comfortable if they are properly scheduled and occur almost around the same time each day.

The main goal is to make your guinea pig comfortable around you as much as possible and to make them enjoy spending time with you. This simply means you will likely spend much time and use lots of food early on as you begin to forge a bond with your pet. They will associate your presence with good things which will help them to overcome their fear of you. Once you earn their confidence and they get used to your presence things begin to fall in place. All fear is gone they are ready for endless cuddles.

8 Basic Training for your Pet Guinea Pig

Guinea pigs are smart animals. With time, patience, consistency and a clear idea of what you want, you can teach your charming little creature some super cute command. Training them is crucial to make your companionship a worthwhile venture for both of you.

A trained guinea pig is a better guinea pig. They are motivated by food, so treats can be used to easily get them to do a ton of things.

Training process

First, you will need to develop a strong bond with your pet. A stable relationship is an important foundation for training. If this is not there it will be pretty difficult to get the attention of your pet.

Every guinea pig has a different taste, so find out the favorite meal of your guinea pig. The idea is to reward them with food every time they do a trick or performs to your expectations.

Decide what trick you want your pet to learn and organize them starting from the simplest. It's much more effective to gradually introduce the training bit by bit, than it is all at once.

 Guinea pigs learn much better and faster if you are working with them consistently on a regular schedule at their pace. Set the time for the training daily and keep to this. Remember the shorter the better. Also, keeping a regular schedule is good for both of you as it will come to be more of a regular routine over time.

Give a reward the moment he performs to expectation and never scold or punish when he makes a mistake or fails to get along with you. Remember mistakes are part of the learning process. Give the reward immediately he does it well to pin his attention to the desired behavior. If you don't do it immediately he may not understand why you're rewarding him, and won't learn to repeat the behavior. Keep the training short and simple. Make it a fun activity. Always stay positive and use positive reinforcement. Give a name to every trick for easy association. One short word is enough. Don't try to teach two different tricks with the same word, this can be confusing.

When you give the command, make sure you guide him through it for him to have an understanding of what it meant. After a few trials, he will be able to match your word with the appropriate action.

Training Tips summary

- Build a strong bond. A stable relationship is an important foundation for training.

- Always use favorite treat of your guinea pig for training to get quick result.

- Give a reward the moment he performs to expectation and never scold or punish when he makes a mistake or gets it wrong.

- Make the training session a fun activity. Always stay positive and use positive reinforcement and have realistic expectations.

- Allow the guinea pig to dictate the pace and keep training sessions relatively short, generally between 8-10 minutes long (depending on your guinea pig's ability)

- If your guinea pig gets confused at a new trick, repeat the exercises until the he clearly knows the trick well.

- If you get frustrated due to low response, stop the training session and come back to it later.

- As usual, try to end every training session on a good note.

- Use nonverbal cues mostly over voice commands whenever possible. Most animals respond much better to nonverbal cues.

- Repetition is the key when teaching your guinea pigs. Keep practicing new tricks until the guinea pig clearly demonstrates a clear understanding.

There are tons lot of thingd you can teach your guinea pigs it all depends on your patience and the ability of your guinea pig. Here are just some of the cool tricks you can teach them.

Litter Box Training

Litter training guinea pigs can have significant benefits. It helps to keep the cage neater and reduces the regular efforts of trying to keep up with the never-ending cleaning. Litter training guinea pigs is not always reliable as it is not always easy to achieve 100% success. The good thing is that you can successfully improve their liter habit by minimizing the tendency of using the whole cage as their litter box. Some guinea pigs can be trained easily, whereas others might not be able to learn, the success rate depends on the personality of your pet. Some of the tips below may also help litter train your pet.

Choose a litter box that is suitable for your guinea pig. An ideal sized litter box for a guinea pig should be big enough for them to easily get in and turn around. Use a different material for the litter box for your guinea pig to differentiate the liter area and the rest part of the cage and make sure that it isn't so dirty that your guinea pig won't want to sit in it. Figure out where he normally does the thing. Guinea pigs will typically urinate in the same spot most of the time. Set the litter box in that area to pin his attention to the spot. Teach him to jump into the litter box. Lure him into the litter box and reward when he jumps in. Practice several times and continue to reward him for staying in the box as well.

Put a handful of hay inside the box, along with a few fecal pellets to keep the guinea pig coming back to the litter box and staying there for at least a few minutes at a time.

If you keep an eye on your guinea pig, and catch him going into the litter box on his own, then immediately reward it with a treat. This action will create an association between using the litter box and being rewarded. It will help pin his attention to the spot and he is likely to perform the action again.

Come When Called

You can attach a name to your pet and make him respond to the name when you call. This is one of the easiest and most necessary tricks you should teach your pet. As earlier stated bonding with your pet is the foundation for all other things. Before you start this particular training, make sure he is not by your side. He may be in his cage or anywhere he can hear and probably see you. Hold out a treat and call him by the name you want. Give the food as soon as he responds. Next, hold out the treat from a few inches away, then say his name and wait for him to come to you. Repeat the exercise by gradually moving farther and farther steps away. When you call his name, offer a treat once he responds to you after you have called his name.

Go Home

Training your guinea pig to go to their cage at your command is another important skill for your guinea pig. To teach your cavy this crucial skill, just toss some delicious snacks into his cage while he is watching. Then, tell him to go home or say the words you like to express this. Repeat the exercise until your pet goes into his cage on command.

Doing a 360-degree turn

Get a cylindrical shaped object and set it in the training area. It can be any color and any type, just makes sure it is safe for your pet. Ensure it stands well so that your guinea doesn't easily knock it over during the training process. The idea is to use a treat to lure him around the object. Hold a treat out in front of him and once you have his attention, move your hand round the object gradually. Once the circle is complete tell him to 'Turn Circles' or any word you may decide to use and then hand over the treat.

Repeat the process until your guinea pig becomes comfortable with the exercise. When you think he has mastered the trick, you can then start giving him the vocal command before you hold out the treat.

Standing up

Most guinea pigs are delightful to watch when they stand up on their hind legs and beg. Standing up is one of the simplest tricks to teach. Start out by holding a treat above the head of the guinea pig just high enough so that he has to stand up to get it. Bring the treat toward his mouth and begin to raise it up slowly so that the guinea pig has to stand on its back feet to get it. The moment he stands on his back legs, don't forget to say the word "stand up' and then give him his reward. Then wait until it stands up a little higher, and by the end wait for him to be standing entirely on its hind legs before he gets rewarded. Remember that the trick is mastered when he can stand at your command without waiting for your reward.

There are tons of things you can teach your pet guinea pigs. It all depends on your patience and how well you can manage them. You should not hesitate to try any tricks you so wish as long as they are entertaining for both of you.

9 Common Guinea Pig Health Problems

Guinea pigs are usually healthy animals, but like any other pet animal; they can be susceptible to specific diseases and conditions. Knowing a number of illnesses that commonly affect them will help you well equiped to handle the issue before they cause problems for your pet.

Some of the problems can be very serious and will require veterinary advice and treatment. Others can be prevented and treated at home with good pet care management.

Preventive Measure

The best way to stop your guinea pig health issues is to prevent them from happening. And the best way to do this is to keep a close watch on your pet. There are areas you can check on a daily basis, to ensure your pets remain healthy. This daily checks will get you familiar with your guinea pigs and detect any physical changes. A healthy guinea pig should be active, and able to move around with no signs of stiffness or difficulty.

Guinea Pig Bottoms

The bottom area of your guinea pig should be clean and dry. Any wetness or smell is a sign of urine infection.

Guinea Pig Coats

Guinea pig hair should be dense, clean and shiny with no sores or bald patches. The presence of sores or bald patches is a sign of parasite infection. Mites and lice cause excessive body scratching. As soon as you spot the problem, get it treated.

Guinea Pig Eyes and Noses

A Guinea pig's eye should be clear and bright. There should be no cloudiness or discharge. Any discharge or cloudiness may indicate an eye infection. Similarly, a guinea pig's nose should be clean, and not runny. Any discharge may suggest infection such as a cold. Any nose or eye problems require urgent veterinary attention.

Guinea Pigs Feet

Guinea pigs' feet are sensitive; you need to check the bottom regularly for signs of soreness.

Monitor any changes and speak with your veterinarian immediately if you suspect there might be issues for concern. Also, make sure your guinea pig is eating and expelling normally. Wash your hands thoroughly before and after handling them. Freeze your pet's bedding and food before use, and keep it away from drafts.

Dental Problems

Guinea pigs' teeth grow continuously which makes them prone to a number of dental issues. The most common cause is misaligned teeth, which can be hereditary or occur because of malnutrition, vitamin C deficiency, or injury. Sometimes guinea pigs with this problem will eat less because chewing can become quite painful. It can also make them develop overly long teeth and experience repeated infections in the mouth. You can manage the issue by having your pet's teeth trimmed regularly by a veterinarian.

Scurvy (Vitamin C Deficiency)

Guinea pigs do not produce vitamin C naturally; they are prone to Scurvy a disease which is caused by lack of vitamin C. Sign of scurvy include loss of appetite, a rough coat, weight loss, lack of energy. Limping and diarrhea are some other symptoms. Scurvy can be deadly, so it should be taken very seriously. To prevent scurvy, make sure that your guinea pig pellets contain vitamin C and are used within 2-3 months of the date of manufacturing. Sometimes Guinea pigs have trouble absorbing enough vitamin C from food and must be given vitamin C supplements directly.

Respiratory Problems

Respiratory problems are probably the most common health complaint in pet guinea pigs. They are sensitive to cold air drafts and can easily develop an upper respiratory infection. A variety of viruses and bacteria may be responsible for this. A cavy having a respiratory issue may experience sneezing, discharge from the nose and/or eyes, loss of appetite and other related illnesses.

Good pet management practices can help prevent the problem. To minimize the likelihood of contacting the disease keep the cage clean and be sure to place it in a draft-free area. Also wash your hands after handling other animals, including guinea pigs at pet stores and quarantining any new addition to the fold.

Pneumonia

Pneumonia is generally caused by a bacterial infection and it is one of the deadliest diseases. Some of the symptoms include trouble breathing, discharge from the nose or mouth, wheezing, weight loss, reddish eyes, and depression. If you think your guinea pig might be suffering from pneumonia, you must contact your vet with immediate effect.

Ectoparasites

Mites, lice, and fleas

Guinea pigs are susceptible to parasites such as mites, lice, and fleas. They are responsible for nearly all the skin problems common with guinea pigs. Signs of infection are scratching and loss of hair. Guinea pigs can transmit these parasites to each other and can also get them from their food and bedding. The good thing is that they can be easily treated or avoided. Lice and their eggs can be typically seen in the bald patches behind the guinea pig's ears and the mites can be seen with a microscope all over the body. The best way to prevent infection is by good pet management. Always keep their housing clean and don't overcrowd them in cages.

Parasites under the skin

Ringworm

Ringworm is among the parasite that lives under the skin of the guinea pigs. It is a fungal infection. Symptoms can include crusty lesions on the skin and excessive itching and even hair loss. Using anti-fungal medication is the best treatment for the disease.

Gastrointestinal Tract Problems

Guinea pigs have very sensitive guts and need to carefully balance the bacterial flora in their gastrointestinal tracts. They can become constipated easily if not fed correctly. They can also develop diarrhea. Both are dangerous and can be life-threatening if not treated immediately.

Constipation makes it difficult for your guinea pig to excrete. You may also observe a lack of feces in the cage, a bloated abdomen or lethargy.

You can prevent constipation by feeding your guinea pig the right diet. Ensure you provide fresh vegetables and clean water every day.

Diarrhea

Diarrhea can be very serious for your cavy's health. It shows up in guinea pig as loose or runny stools, and messiness underneath the tail. Diarrhea can often be accompanied by dehydration and hypothermia, both of which can be dangerous if not treated immediately.

To prevent diarrhea, keep the cage clean and give your pet the correct diet. If you have to change the diet make sure you introduce new foods gradually.

If your guinea pigs show any signs of constipation or diarrhea. You need to visit the vets to ensure that the correct care is given.

Urinary problems

Guinea pigs are susceptible to urinary stones that often form in their kidney or bladder. They cause aching and discomfort in your pet. Symptoms include infrequent urination, a hunched posture, and bloody urine. In most cases, bladder stone problems often need urgent medical attention. Early signs of urinary problems must always be referred to your veterinary for a thorough examination.

Uterine and Ovarian Diseases

Spaying your female guinea pig can prevent uterine and ovarian diseases. Also if you keep both sexes it will ensure population control and prevent multiple litters of guinea pigs. Females often develop uterine and ovarian problems.

Foot Sores

Guinea pigs can develop sore hocks which are common with caged animals. It is a result of heavy abrasion of the feet and can occur more frequently in overweight guinea pigs. Their hind feet become inflamed and swollen on the bottoms, and they lose some of their hair. The problem can cause pain and lameness if not treated on time. If you think he might be suffering from this condition take him to the vet right away. The vet may give you antibiotic ointment to put on the legs. To prevent further occurrence, change your cage flooring by providing them with solid flooring.

Lumps

Lumps on a pet guinea pig skin can be caused by a number of different problems, including an abscess or a tumor.

An abscess is a bacterial infection usually resulting from an injury. You may need to visit your vet to drain the abscess or surgically remove it.

Tumors can be gentle or cancerous and are totally harmless and can be removed in a simple surgical process.

To prevent the disease, always examine your guinea pig every day for early detection. If you suspect any lump take him to a veterinarian immediately for a diagnosis.

About the Author

Dave is a pet lover. He was first introduced to the world of rabbits and cavies at an early age when he owned and raised them as a hobby. His burning desire to help **beginners** led him to put together this **essential guide to guinea pig's ownership, care, and training.** Dave lives at home with his wife and three children where they spend much of their spare time looking after their adorable pets.